# SYMPTOMS OF PLANT DISEASE

# SYMPTOMS OF PLANT DISEASE

*By*

**Dr. Sumia Fatima**
*M.Sc., Ph.D., F.S.Sc., F.S.L.Sc.*
*Professor and Head*
*Dept. of Botany*
*Dr. Rafiq Zakaria College for Women*
*Jublee Park, Aurangabad - 431 001*
*Maharashtra (India)*

*&*

**Mr. Yogesh C. Khot**
*Dept. of Botany*
*Devgiri College of Arts, Science & Commerce*
*Aurangabad - 431 001*
*Maharashtra (India)*

DPH

DISCOVERY PUBLISHING HOUSE PVT. LTD.
NEW DELHI-110 002

*Published by:*
**Namit Wasan**
**DISCOVERY PUBLISHING HOUSE PVT. LTD.**
4383/4B, Ansari Road, Darya Ganj
New Delhi-110 002 (India)
*Phone* : +91-11-23279245, 43596064-65
*Fax* : +91-11-23253475
*E-mail* : discoverypublishinghouse@gmail.com
namitwasan9@gmail.com
sales@discoverypublishinggroup.com
*web* : www.discoverypublishinggroup.com

*First Edition:* **2016**

**ISBN: 978-93-5056-781-4**

**Symptoms of Plant Disease**



*Printed at:*
Infinity Imaging Systems
Delhi

# Preface

The book covers the entire field of symptomatology of plant pathogenic organisms such as fungi, bacteria, virus, Mycoplasma and nematodes. Almost all types of symptoms caused by different groups of pathogenic organisms are covered. The symptomatology associated with mineral deficiencies and adverse environmental factors has been discussed in detail. Easy understanding of terminology of symptoms of plant diseases is very important to manage the crop plant diseases. The disease is any abnormal condition of plants structure which may be visible in the form of symptoms. The abnormal condition of plant is the result of interaction of pathogenic organism with host tissue. A symptom is a visible and detectable expression of structural or physiological abnormality of plant. The symptoms often involve changes in form, colour, odour, texture of infected plant. The infected plant shows various types of symptoms due to interaction of pathogenic living organism or non-living causal agent. The non-pathogenic causal agents are deficiency or excess of minerals and adverse environmental factors. The book covers description of 56 types of symptoms caused by fungi, 25 types of symptoms caused by bacteria, 23 types of symptoms caused by viruses, 12 types of symptoms caused by nematode, 16 types of symptoms caused by Mycoplasma, 15 types of symptoms caused by physiological disorders and many types of symptoms caused by air pollutants, high or low temperature, light, freezing injury, mineral deficiency and adverse effect of environment.

This is the first book of the world written only on symptomatology of plant pathogens responsible for the plant diseases of economically important food crops. This book is useful to the students and teachers and researchers of plant science, horticulture and agriculture, botany and plant pathology.

**Dr. Sumia Fatima**
**Mr. Yogesh C. Khot**

# Contents

# 1 Introduction

Study of symptoms of infected plant caused by biotic or abiotic causal agents is termed as symptomatology. Symptomatology is the study of visible change in the plant or plant part due to the infection of parasitic or non-parasitic living or non-living causal agent. The purpose of this book is to develop practical understanding of symptomatology for use in disease diagnosis of plants. The diseases are recognized largely by a specific characteristic signs which are called as symptoms. Easy understanding of terminology of symptomatology is very important to manage the crop plant diseases. The disease is any abnormal condition of plants structure which may be visible in the form of symptoms. The abnormal condition of plant is the result of interaction of pathogenic organism with host tissue. The pathogenic organisms are host specific or host organ specific in nature. Pathogenic organisms develop a specific type of symptoms in presence of proper host plant during favorable environmental conditions. A symptom is a visible and detectable expression of structural or physiological abnormality of plant. The symptoms often involve changes in form, colour, odour, texture of infected plant. The infected plant shows various types of symptoms due to interaction of pathogenic living organism of non-pathogenic harmful causal agent. The non-pathogenic causal agents are deficiency or excess of minerals and adverse environmental factors. Any change in the plant due to pathogenic organism is termed as disease. In case of entophytic organisms, the mycelial threads and spores of pathogenic organism are visible external to the affected plant part. The pathogenic organisms which are visible on the infected host plant part are termed as 'ectoparasites'. Those pathogenic organisms which causes disease to the plant but not visible on to the host surface are termed as endoparasites. In case of endophytic parasitic organisms the pathogen invades the plant tissue which is expressed by a variety of symptoms. Each type of pathogen produces a specific type of symptoms. On the basis of symptoms it is easy to identify the type of disease. The symptoms may possess variable colours, sizes, shapes and developmental patterns.

In India there is great variation in soil type and all other environmental factors, hence it is highly favourable for the growth and development of many types of varieties of plants. (Schumann, & D'Arcy, (2010). The plants get affected by fungal, bacterial, viral, Mycoplasma and nematodal pathogens which affect the growth and development of plants. The pathogenic organisms cause a variety of structural biochemical and physiological changes into the respective host plants. The structural changes caused due to interaction of pathogenic fungi and host tissue expressed in the form of a specific signs that are termed as symptoms.

The non-required change in plant is induced by the pathogenic or saprophytic organism which is expressed by development of different types of signs which are visible on affected plants is termed as symptoms and the phenomenon is termed as symptomatology. There are many types of symptoms caused due to pathogenic organisms in the affected fruits. The symptoms are developed due to destruction of affected tissue or due to biochemical changed induced by the pathogen into the host plant. Symptoms are visibly changes in size, shape or colour of affected plant part or changes in normal functioning of plant due to interaction host, pathogen and environmental factors. (San Blas and Calderone, (2008).

The disease symptoms are very important evidence used in management, although detailed information about environmental and cultural factors must be considered as well. The exact role of symptoms in diagnosis of diseases is different. Symptom can be a key point to identify the disease and causal organism. However, one must be very careful in evaluating them since they may belong to secondary organisms or saprophytic organisms. The symptoms cannot indicate how the disease develops after development of pathogen inside the host tissue. But a type of symptom gives an idea about the type of disease by its specific expressions of the pathogen. The symptoms support more complete interpretation and evaluation of diseases and thereby contribute both to diagnosis and to the prescription of more effective integrated control measures.

The symptoms occur singly or in group there is great variation in occurrence of each type of symptoms. The expression of symptom may vary from indistinct to more distinct that depends on intensity of the development of diseases. The disease intensity directly correlated with environmental factors and host susceptibility. The symptoms caused by physiological disorders are totally different than the symptoms caused by any living pathogenic organism. The symptoms may be visible or non-visible (physiological disorder), may be more distinct or indistinct. The terms used to explain symptom according to their occurrence, appearance and its all external and internal features. The plant pathologist classified plant diseases on the basis of symptoms.

The change in plant is induced by the pathogen which is expressed by formation of different types of signs which are visible on affected plant part are termed as symptoms. The types of symptoms caused due to pathogenic organisms in the affected host plant are discussed above. The symptoms are developed due to destruction of affected tissue or due to biochemical changed induced by the pathogen into the host cells (Webster and Weber, 2007). Symptoms in any visible change in size, shape or colour of host plant or change in normal functioning of plant, due to interaction host, pathogen and environmental of factors together.

On the basis of different types of symptoms the plant diseases are classified into different groups. The symptoms developed by fungal plant pathogens in the respective host possess inter-cellular or intra-cellular mycelium.

The mildew causing pathogenic fungi spread over external surface of affect host plant part. The mycelium must be necked or endophytic. Rust fungi produce group of spores which become necked in the form of small pustules. The smut disease causing fungi produce different types of fruiting bodies such as sclerotic or ergot body. Leaf spot disease causing fungi plant (White, et al, 2006). The spots vary greatly in size, shape and colour. The visible symbols occur on infected plant due to biotic or non-biotic entities are termed as symptoms.

The general characters of the fungi are:

1. The fungal flora has been adopted to be alive in broad spectrum of environmental variation.
2. The fungi are extensively available in infected hosts, air, water and soil.
3. The fungi include fairly familiar organisms such as mushrooms, toadstools, puffballs and the bracket fungi that grow on tree trunks.
4. There are also the mould fungi which are very important which grow on stale bread, cheese, fruit or other food.
5. Many of the mould fungi live on organic matter in soil or in dead wood.
6. Fungi are devoid of chlorophyll hence survived as a saprophyte or a parasite.
7. The yeasts are the single celled fungi similar to the moulds in some respects.
8. Some fungal species are parasites and live in other organisms particularly plants, where they cause diseases that can affect the crop plants.

9. Many fungi are not made up of cells but of microscopic threads called 'hyphae'.
10. The network of thread like hyphae constitutes the body of fungus which is known as 'mycelium'.
11. The fungal thread which possesses cross walls are termed as 'septate hyphae' and the fungal threads without cross walls are termed as 'coenocytic hyphae'.
12. The cross walls of hyphae may have large pores through which cytoplasm flow takes place.
13. The cross walls divided the hyphal thread into cell like regions.

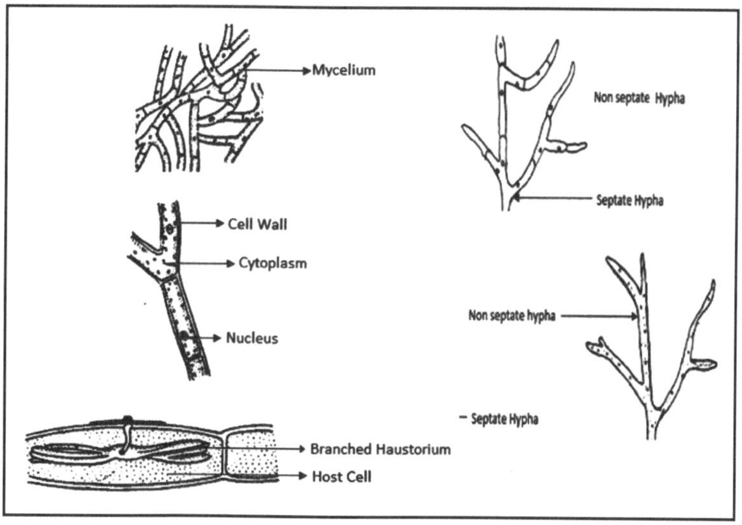


**The Fungal Hyphae**

14. In the hyphae which do have cross walls (septa) that are termed as 'septate hyphae'.
15. There may be one or two or many nuclei in each compartment of septate hypha.
16. In the species without septa, the nuclei are distributed throughout the cytoplasm.
17. The hyphae are like microscopic tubes which are filled with cytoplasm and vacuole at the centre.

18. The cytoplasm contains organelles, lipid droplets, or granules of glycogen but unlike plants.
19. There are no chloroplasts and starch grains in the hyphal threads of any fungi.
20. The hyphal wall may contain cellulose or chitin or both.
21. The chitin is similar to cellulose but the chitin molecule contains nitrogen atom.
22. The hyphae of saprophytic fungi secretes enzymes into the organic material and digest it to liquid products and the digested products are then absorbed back in to the hyphae and used for energy.
23. The fungi reproduce by releasing microscopic, single celled spores (asexual reproduction).

# 2 Symptoms caused by Fungi

There are varieties of fungi cause the varieties of plant diseases. The fungi consist of septate or non-septate hyphae. These are endo- or ecto-parasites. The parasitic fungus infects the plants and causes diseases. The fungi are hosted specific in nature. The fungal pathogens produce different types of symptoms after infection.

The entry of pathogen into the host plant takes place through stomata, or hydathodes or insect injuries or through soft part of host by mechanical pressure. After entry into the host, the pathogen grows into the intercellular space that absorbs food from host tissue by sending sucking organs (haustoria) into the host cells. Pathogenic fungi are the filamentous living parasitic organisms. Thallus in filamentous or thread like. The fungal thread is termed as 'hyphae'. There are two types of hyphae, i.e. septate and non-septate. These are cosmopolitan in occurrence. They are host specific in nature, and causes a variety of symptoms and great losses of crop yield. The fungal parasites produce different types of symptoms like leaf spots, powdery mildews, blast, chlorosis, downey mildews, blight, rot, wilts, seedling blight, bunt, ergot, anthracnose etc. (Sinclair and Hudler, 2005).

The example of fungal diseases are kernel bunt (*Tilletia indica*), blast of rice (*Pyricularia oryzae*), rust of wheat (*Puccinia graminis*), brown spot of rice (*Helminthosporium oryzae*), downey mildew of rice (*Sclerophthora macrospora*), ergot of *bajra* (*Claviceps fusiformis*), pigeon pea blight (*Phytopthora drechsleri*), wilt of cotton (*Fusarium oxysporum f sp.vasinfectum*), late blight of potato (*Phytopthora drechsleri*), Phomopsis blight of brinjal (*Phomopsis vexans*), Penicillium rot of *amla* (*Penicillium italicum*), apple scab (*Venturia inaquilis*), etc. Rusts, Smuts, Mildews, Root Rots, Blight, Leaf spots, Wilts, Cankers, Fruit rots, Dieback, Chlorosis, Galls, Hypertrophy, Curl, Phyllody, Witches broom, Damping off, Streaks, Blotch, Necrosis, Stripe and Anthracnose.

**Symptoms caused by Fungi**

1. Anthracnose
2. Atrophy
3. Black shank
4. Blast
5. Blight
6. Blisters
7. Blotch
8. Bunt
9. Black scarf
10. Cavity spot
11. Shelling
12. Damping off diseases
13. Die-back
14. Grain mould
15. Gummosis
16. Hypertrophy
17. Hydrosis
18. Leaf spot
19. Shot hole
20. Leaf weathering
21. Leaf drooping
22. Black point
23. Blast
24. Defoliation
25. Chlorosis
26. Necrosis
27. Stripe
28. Mildew
29. Proliferation
30. Pitting
31. Rot diseases
32. Tumefaction
33. Shoestrings
34. Puckering
35. Russet
36. Callus
37. Malformation
38. Dwarfing or stunting
39. Gigantism
40. Mould
41. Rust
42. Resinosis

43. Smuts
44. Green ear
45. Ergot
46. Smudge
47. Scab
48. Stem gall
49. Wire stem
50. Black leg
51. Black scarf
52. Stag head
53. Shanking
54. Wilt
55. Club root
56. Pink root
57. Hairy root
58. Vascular discolouration
59. Wart
60. Fly speak
61. Decline
62. Felt disease
63. Grassy stunt
64. Witches broom
65. Black bundle
66. Flattening of branches
67. White tip

**Anthracnose**

There is a broad spectrum of a variety of crop plants fruit crops, medicinal plants and forest trees are susceptible to fungi causing anthracnose disease. It appears on all aerial parts of infected plant. These are symptoms which appear rough in touch. The affected region show brick red to purplish red coloration. The spots are of various sizes and of various colours i.e. black, brown or reddish in colour that varies according to the plant part infected. Anthracnose affects the photosynthetic activity of leaves; restrict the growth and healthy development of plant. The infected fruits show rot during transportation and storage periods. The disease affects the quality of vegetables. The infected fruits and vegetables become unfit for consumption. Exm: Anthracnose of mango caused by *Colletotrichum gloesporioides*. Anthracnose of pea pods caused by *Colletotrichum sp.* The anthracnose (necrotic spots) at maturity shows visible tiny black coloured structures called acervuli which are randomly distributed on the necrotic region. Jonathan, *et.al*, (2012).

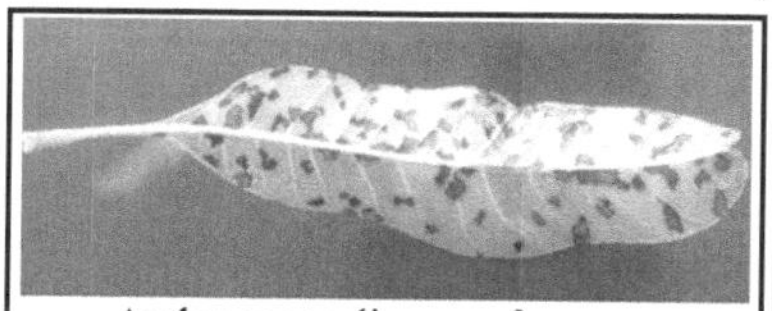

Anthracnose disease of mango

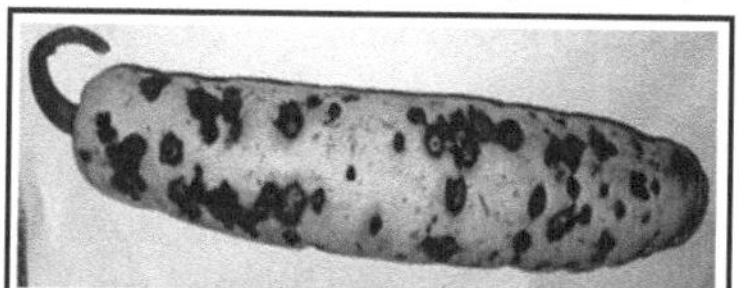

Anthracnose symptoms on bottle guard

### Atrophy

Mostly the symptoms are visible at growing region of infected host. Atrophy is the symptom in which infection of pathogen restricts the cell division especially at the growing region of plant. The affected plant remains short. The infected parts of plant show suppressed growth. Such types of symptoms are termed as atrophy. Atrophy symptoms are caused by fungal pathogens. The sarso plants show suppressed floral part due to infection of *Pernospora brassicae* (Zieslin and Halevy, 2006). The infected plant becomes abnormally small or incomplete. Such symptoms are termed as atrophy.

### Black Shank

The disease occurs as small necrotic brown coloured spots on the leaf. The spots are distinct on both the surfaces of infected leaf. The spots also occur on leaflets, rachis and petiole. Many spots increase in size which cover entire surface of leaf. The adjacent leaves also get infected. The heavily infected leaves get curled off and turn brown. The lesions on the lower surface of the leaf show growth of the parasitic fungus (Thomas and Ramakrishnan, 1948). The infected plant shows dark black coloured spots which are scattered all over the infected host. On stems it produces patches of irregular margins. The infections also extend to the root system. The infected region gets shriveled. The black shank disease of tobacco is caused by *Phytopthora parasitica* var. *nicotianae* (Breda de Haan) Tucker.

### Blast

The symptoms of blast disease restricted to the leaves. In severe cases of disease development typical symptoms appear on all other parts i.e. in leaf sheath, node, rachis and glumes. The leaf show small water soaked flecks which measure about 3 mm in diameter. These spots increase rapidly to attain the size of about one centimeter broad. The spots appear spindle shaped. The centre of spot may be grayish green and the boarder may have dark brown colour. There is a distinct yellow halo present around each spot. In susceptible varieties the entire leaf killed due to formation of numerous lesions. Similar lesions develop on leaf sheath. The disease makes the plants unhealthy, infected leaves dry up, stems become thin and yellowish. The productivity of plant gets affected. Nodal infection occurs in mature plants. Nodes break off easily. The peduncles of flowers show infection of pathogen in the form of dark brown to black spot. The grains poorly develop and panicle remains erect. If the panicle is infected late, there is partial grain filling. Infected glumes possess dark brown to black spots. The infection to seedling result into burnt appearance. It reduces yield of crop, hence it is a economically important disease (Kumar and Yadav, 2012). The pathogenic fungus responsible for blast disease of rice is *Pyricularia grisea*

**Blight**

These are very much destructive symptoms caused by fungal, bacterial pathogen, adverse environmental factors or due to mineral deficiency. Mostly blight symptoms appear on leaf, stem, and fruits except root system. Initially the infected leaf show small round or irregular shaped spots. Gradually the spots increase in size. By the time many spots coalesce to form a large blighted area. Blight is the symptoms which occupy larger portion of leaf; the affected regions possess dead cells because of interaction of pathogen and host, (Rathore, 2006). Management of diseases of green gram with fungicides. '*Indian Journal of Mycology and Plant Pathology* 36: 138-141'. It causes death and dropping off of affected leaves. The blight diseases of host leaf caused by the group of fungi which belonging to class fungi imperfecti. Seed, soil and air are the main sources of inoculums of the

Leaf blight symptoms

pathogen. The blight symptoms are not only restricted to leaf, but are also developed on stem and fruit surface due to interaction of respective pathogens. The fungi causing blight diseases of a variety of plants are host specific in nature. The mycoflora causing blight diseases in plants are: *Ascochaeta, Colletotrichum, Phoma, Gloeosporium, Phmopsis, Phyllosticta, Cercospora, Diplodia, Septoria, Batryodiplodia Alternaria,* and *Helminthosporium.* In case of leaf blight larger portion of leaf is occupied by pathogenic organisms, causing death of cells. In some cases, the leaf spots increase in size and get mixed and large blighted areas are formed. Exm: Early blight of potato (*Alternaria solani*), leaf blight of wheat (*Alternaria triticina*).

Types of blight symptoms on the basis of infected plant part:

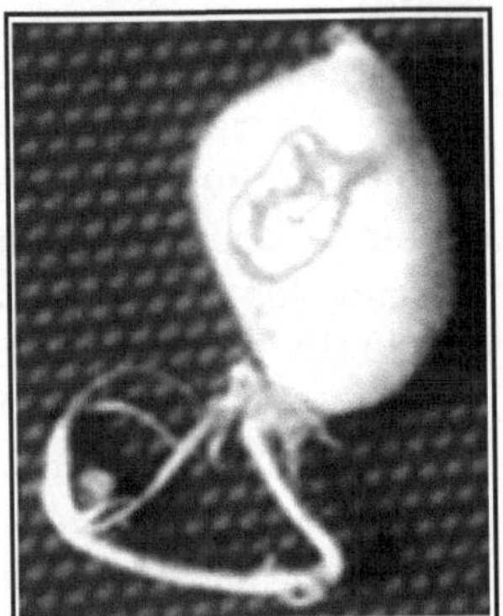

**Pod blight of Gram**

1. Sheath blight of rice – *Rhizoctonia solani*
2. Leaf blight of wheat – *Alternaria triticina*
3. Fire blight of apple – *Erwinia amylowora*
4. Early blight of potato – *Alternaria solani*
5. Late blight of potato – *Phytopthora infestans*
6. Web blight of bean (*Rhizotonia solani*)
7. Halo blight of bean is caused by *Pseudomonas syringae*
8. Pod blight of gram- *Ascochaeta rabae*
9. Stem blight of *Cajanus cajan*- *Phytopthora drechsleri*

*Leaf blight*

Initially symptoms develop as a small, spherical spots on leaf surface which are yellowish in colour. The spot gradually becomes somewhat rectangular in shape. The spots increase in size and coal sac to involve most of the area of leaf. Infected patches are spread in the form of longitudinal streaks on leaf surface. The affected tissue becomes blackish brown in colour due to interaction of endophytic fungus, (Agros, (2005). Moist environment is highly favourable for development of disease. Heavily infected leaves dry up. It affects photosynthetic activity of plant. Dried leaves hang down. Yield is greatly reduced. In severe cases of disease development all the leaves become blighted. The leaf blight disease of maize is caused by *Helminthosporium turcicum* Passerini.

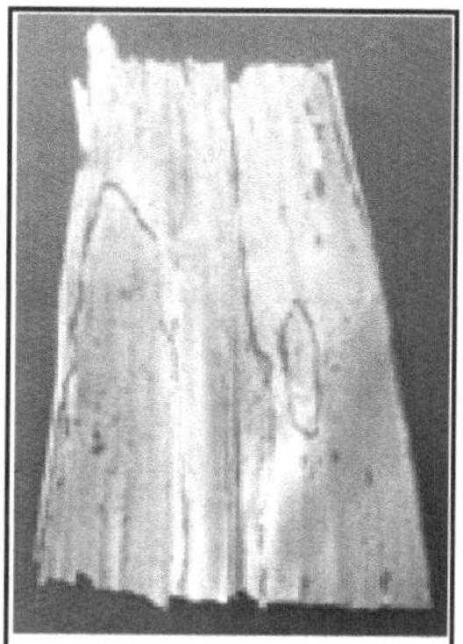

**Blight of Leaf**

*Stem Blight*

Blight disease is a serious disease of the pigeon pea. The plants grown in stagnant water for longer duration gets infected by soil borne pathogen. The symptoms are visible on stem just above the soil surface. The infected region of stem get swelled which becomes larger than normal thickness, (Singh, 1998). All the stages of plant growth are highly susceptible for infection of the pathogen. Infection to seedlings show crust like growth at the girdle region. Initially seedling possesses water soaked lesion which later on change to rough crust like and the seedling turns yellow and collapse. The infected leaves become yellowish. The stem of mature plants dries up. The stem blight disease of pigeon pea is caused by *Phytopthora drechsleri* f. sp. *cajani.*

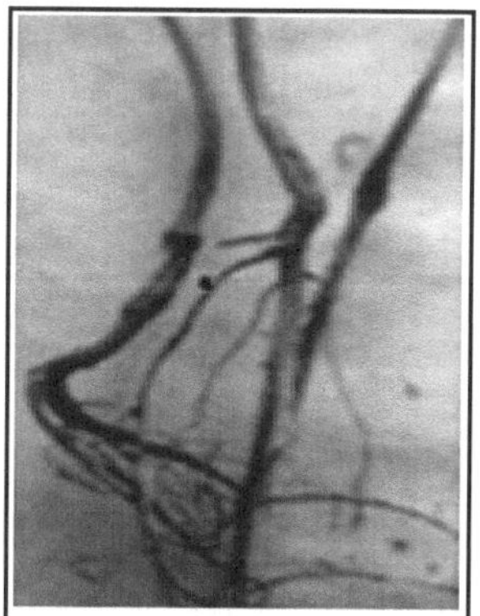

**Stem Blight of *Cajanus cajan***

*Ray Blight*

The blight symptoms initiated and developed on ray florets of *Chrysanthemum*, hence the diseases are termed as ray blight. The ray florets are attacked and their blooms are deformed and become one sided. The inner florets also get attacked and resulted into black rot. The leaves and stem shows brown lesions. Infected plant shows stunted growth.

*Web Blight*

Leaf web blight of bean leaf is caused by *Rhizoctonia solani.* Initially a small light green water soaked spots appear on mature leaf, which increase gradually involving most of the area of leaf. The spots are of variable in size and shape; which are reddish brown in colour. The affected region shows interwoven hyphae which appear like a web. Numerous sclerotia also associated with hyphal threads. In severe cases of disease development, defoliation is common.

*Sheath Blight*

The spots of dead areas develop on leaf sheath which increase in size. The affected leaf gets dried and fell off. It causes heavy loss of yield. The young tillers also get infected. The disease especially occur on sheath first, hence the disease is termed as sheath blight.

*Fire Blight*

The symptoms resemble a burned area, which turns black, shrunken and even cracks are developed; hence the blight is termed as fire blight. The fire blight of pear tree is a bacterial disease. The pathogenic organism is *Erwinia amylovora.*

*Early Blight*

The early blight symptoms may occur on leaf, fruit, and stem. Initially a very small black spots are developed, which measure about 1-3 mm in diameter. Mostly the spots are brown to black in colour and roughly spherical. In favourable environmental condition the spots coaleaec to form large blighted patches. The spots consist of concentric rings. The spot surrounded by yellow halo is the characteristic feature of early blight symptoms. The early blight diseases of tomato and potato crop are caused by *Alternaria solani.*

*Late Blight*

The late blight symptoms occur on all the parts of plant except root system. At the initial stage a small black spots of

1-2 mm develop on leaf which increase during moist environment. The spots are encircled by yellow halo. Many spots develop on affected leaf which causes drying and defoliation of leaf. Such symptoms affect the yield of crop. The lower surfaces of affected leaf consist of numerous mycelial threads and sporangia. The late blight disease of potato is caused by *Phytopthora infestans.*

*Inflorescence Blight*

The inflorescence of cashew nut attacked by fungal pathogen called as *Gloeosporium mangiferae* and entire inflorescence get dried.

*Chupon Blight*

The symptoms initiate anywhere on the leaf lamina or petiole and gradually extend to the stem. The symptoms mostly start in the axils of the leaves, at the top of twigs or chupons. Initially water soaked, brown lesion develops. When the stem is enriched by the lesion the portion present above the site of infection dies. Severe defoliation may occur during rainy season. Exm: Chupon blight of cocoa is caused by *Phytopthora palmivora.*

*Ashy Stem Blight*

The infected plant shows brown lesions at the collar region. The lesions extend in all direction covering the entire stem and killing the growing points. The vascular tissue turns dark brown in colour. The root let's get rotted. The plant dies and dries up. Such type of symptoms termed as ashy stem blight. Ashy stem blight of bean is caused by *Macrophomina phaseolina.*

*Copper Blight*

The characteristics features of copper blight symptoms are development of yellowish brown spots on leaves which turn copper coloured. The spots are irregular in shapes which are enveloped with a mycelial mat along with dark dot like fruiting bodies (perithecia). Defoliation affects the yield. The copper blight of tea is caused by *Guignardia camelliae.*

### *Blister Blight*

The symptoms develop on young leaf and bud in the form of small, pinkish yellow round spots; the upper surface of leaf show shallow depression. The lower surface bugles with a blister like swellings corresponding to the depression. The pinkish colour turns to deep red. The old spots become powdery and white in colour. Heavily infected leaves droop off. Sometimes leaves show curling and distortion. The blister blight symptoms occur in tea leaf due to infection of *Exobasidium vexans.*

### *Grey Blight*

Initially a small brown spots develops on the elder leaves which soon turn grey. The spots are irregular in margin and many spot coalesce to form large irregular grey patches giving the blighting appearance. Concentric rings are prominent on the spots. The affected region get covered by numerous black coloured fruiting bodies of the fungus. Grey blight symptoms observed in tea plant infected by *Pestalotia theae.*

### *Thread Blight*

In this case the mycelium binds the shoots together. A typical white threads of fungal hyphae pass along the petiole and stems, covering the branch and lower leaf surface with a hyphal web. The white growth of pathogenic fungus spread all over the leaf blade, petiole and at the basal region of the shoot. Thread blight symptoms of tea is caused due to *Pellicularia koleroga.*

## Blisters

Slightly raised symptoms which occur on infected plant part are termed as blisters. The blister symptoms are classified on the basis of colour and morphology. Blisters are the raised spots mostly develop on the lower leaf surface due to the infection of pathogenic organism. The blisters on infected leaf greatly variable in colour and texture. The blisters consist of clusters of spores of all age group.

The infected leaf show very small, yellowish spots on lower surface of leaf, which can be distinguished easily. The spots are circular is shape, which increase gradually attaining a size of about 3-10 mm in diameter. On the upper surface of leaf which co-inside the blisters show shallow depression. The fully mature symptoms possess blisters on under surface of leaf which are slightly raised and randomly scattered. There is great variation in size of blisters. The blister consists of pathogenic hyphae which turns white at maturity. (Ajay and Baby, 2010). The surface of blisters show growth of pathogenic fungus and numerous spores. The infected leaves turn yellowish and dry up. Entire leaf lamina including veins show blisters. In severe cases of disease development the blisters are formed on petiole, stem and tender growing shoots. The stem shows grey coloured patches. The stem becomes weak, which can break off easily. The pathogenic fungus responsible for blister blight of tea is *Exobasidium vexans.*

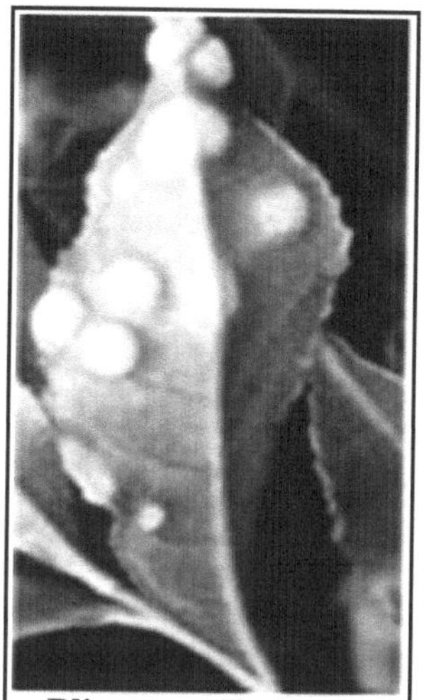

**Blisters on Tea Leaf**

Blisters are the raised spots mostly develop on the lower leaf surface due to the infection of pathogenic organism. The blisters on infected leaf greatly variable in colour and texture. The blisters consist of clusters of spores of all age group.

**White Blisters**

White shining blisters are caused by *Albugo* on variety of plants of family cruciferae. The white coloured blisters caused by *Albugo* are soft in touch that consists of compact arrangement of fungal spores.

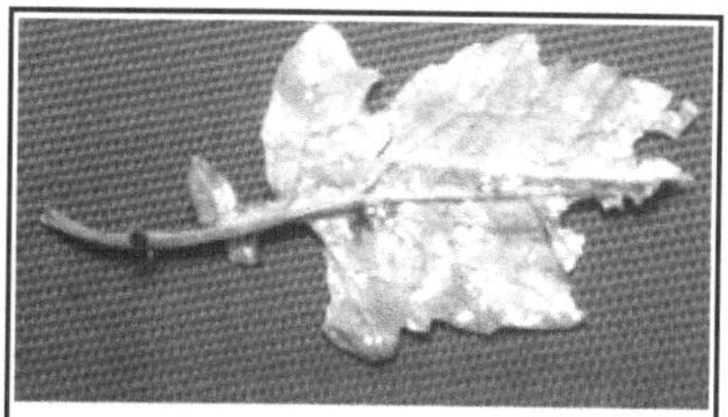

**White Blisters of *Albugo***

**Brown Blisters**

Brown coloured blisters or pustules are mostly caused by *Puccinia* on the leaf of many of the cereal plants such as wheat, jowar, bajra, maize etc. The blisters caused by *Puccinia* are rough in touch that consists of numerous spores. These are also slightly raised appear like a brown dot.

**Blotch**

The spot developed by the pathogen on the respective host leaf surface are sunken with a yellowish zone around it and a clearly purple centre. Many spots increase in size and get mixed, hence a severely affected leaf may have large blighted areas, that extend up to the around petiole. During highly favourable environment, the affected region may have ranked brownish black spores.

*(i)* **Net Blotch:** It is the symptom in which large discoloured or inflammatory patches of irregular margin occur on the leaves of affected leaf. *Pyrenosphora dictyoides* causes net blotch symptoms on grasses.

*(ii)* **Leaf Blotch:** Blotch is a symptom in which discoloured inflamated patches are formed on the leaf of infected plant. Mostly the patches are of irregular margin. The leaf of Podophyllum (*Podophyllum peltata* L.) infected by *Septotinia podophyllina* Whetzel shows blotch symptoms. (Kandikannan, *et.al*, 2008).

*(iii)* **Purple Blotch:** Purple blotch lesions are oval with a well delimited margin between dry infected tissue and the healthy parts of the leaf. The central part of the spot is purple, caused by *Alternaria porri* of garlic. (Miller & Lacy, 1995). Schwortz (2008) reported purple blotch of onion leaf caused by *Alternaria pori* is a highly destructive disease.

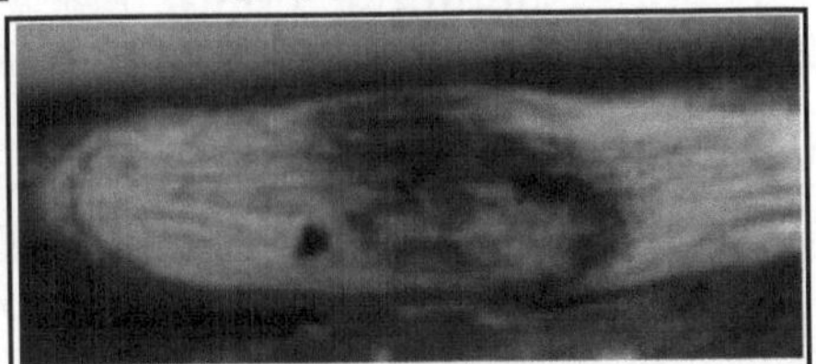

**Purple Blotch of Onion**

The characteristics features of purple blotch symptoms are, the infected leaves of onion possess small sunken spots which possesses yellow zone around it. The spot is slightly elongated, which gradually increase in size involving large area of leaf. The centre of spot is purple in colour. Such types of symptoms are termed blotch. The purple blotch symptoms of onion caused by *Alternaria pori*, a soil or bulb borne or air borne inoculums.

*(iv)* **Big Blotch:** The fungal pathogen *Colletotrichum capsici* (Syd.) Butler & Bisby causes big blotch disease of turmeric leaf (*Curcuma longa*). The infection spread in all direction from the site of main infected area hence it is called big blotch.

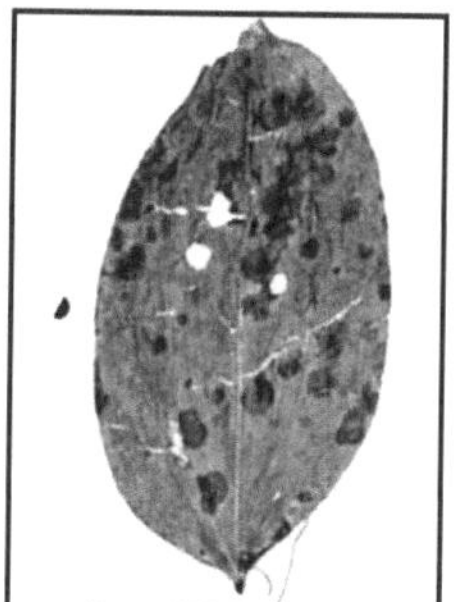
Leaf Blotch of Turmeric

**Bunt**

The pathogen enters the host plant and reaches the ovary. The infection spread in the intercellular space of cells of the infected ovary. Gradually the infection spread the region of entire ovary. In advanced cases of disease development the infected ovary gets replaced by compact mass of fungal mycelium and spores of the pathogen. Such grains covered with silvery membrane which is made up of interwoven hyphal threads. The silvery membrane is called as pericarp. Such symptoms are called bunt (Krishna and Singh 1982).

The bunt disease is very common in most of the cereal crop and grasses. Exm: Karnal bunt disease of wheat (*Neovossia indica).*

*(i)* **Karnal Bunt:** The disease becomes evident only after the emergence of ear and formation of initial stage of grain formation. Certain grains in the ear show Infection. The infected grains transformed to black hard sorus. Sori are

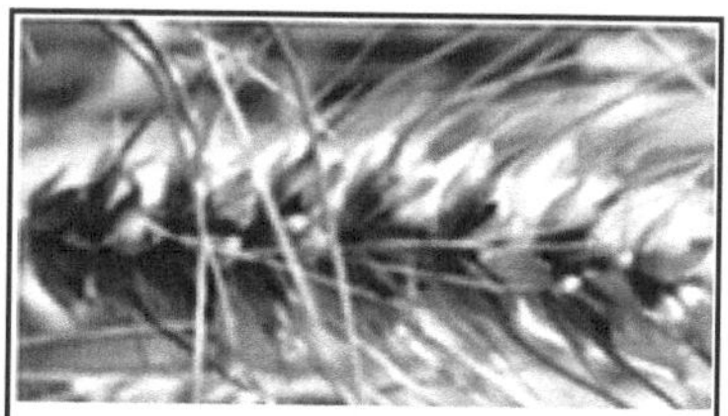
Kernal Bunt of Wheat

randomly distributed in the ear. In the mature ear they are more distinct. The Sori or bunted grains consist of spore balls which remain enveloped by a thin pericarp in early stage. Later on the pericarp gets ruptured and spore balls get exposed. The infected grains emit foul fishy smell. The karnal bunt disease of wheat is caused by *Neovossia indica* (Mundkur, 1940), *Tilletia indica* (Fischer)

**Black Scurf**

The stem canker of potato plant is caused by fungal pathogen called as *Rhizoctonia solani.* The infected stem possesses browning of growing tips. On the mature sprouts, elongated, circular necrotic lesions develop near tubers. The sprouts get killed in severe cases of black scarf disease. When shoots develop from seed potato, the small necrotic spot develop on the stem just above soil surface. The necrotic spot contain dead cells which gradually extend around the stem, which is black in colour and cankerous spot. Such type of symptoms termed as black scurf (Surman 2010).

**Cavity Spot**

The infected carrot with *Pythium violae* produce small lens shaped cavities of 2-1 cm in diameter, which are randomly distributed, on carrot. The large sized lesions easily get ruptured. The cavities consist of hyphal threads. The cavities may have slightly raised border. The spot development initiates at the growing stages of carrot which are retained up to harvest time. Such type of symptoms termed as cavity spot.

**Shelling**

The infected plant show drying of buds or fruit due to interaction of pathogen. The infected bud or fruit drop off before maturity at any stage of its development is termed as shelling.

**Damping off Diseases**

The damping off diseases of seedlings of a variety of plants are very common diseases in sick soil. The damping off of seedlings of forest trees, vegetables, fruit tree are very common in India and throughout the world. The pathogens causing damping off diseases are soil borne or seed borne. The soil or seed borne pathogen becomes active in presence of little moisture. The seed borne pathogen becomes active at the time of germination of seed and spread inside the host tissue resulting seedling rot diseases. If the seedling get rotted before emergence of seedling is termed as pre-emergence damping off. If the seedling get rotted after emergence of seedling is termed as post-emergence damping off. In case of post-emergence damping off the seedling gets rotted just after emergence on soil surface. The infected seedling show water soaked lesion on seedling just above soil surface. Gradually the lesion increase to the girth of seedling. The infected seedlings fell off on the ground. The fungi causing damping off diseases are mostly survive in soil. (Grabowski, 2012). The fungal flora causing damping off diseases of a variety of plants are *Pythium, Rhizoctonia,* and *Phytopthora* etc.

Exm: Damping off of vegetable seedlings (*Pythium aphanidermatum*), (Tredway Lane, et. al., 2011).

*Pre-emergence damping off*

In this case the seedling gets infected in the soil and gets rotted before emergence below the soil surface. This phenomenon is termed as pre-emergence damping off.

*Post-emergence damping off*

The seed germinate and comes out of the soil surface. The radical of seedling get infected by pathogenic fungus found in soil causes soft rot disease of seedling. The infection gradually extends to the delicate stem of the seedling and entire seedling collapse after emergence. This is called as post-emergence damping off.

**Healthy Seedlings**

Quite frequently seedlings in seed beds are completely destroyed by damping off or they die soon after transplantation. Poor seed germination or poor emergence of seedlings is due to damping off infections in pre-emergence stage. Sometimes older plants get killed but they develop root and stem lesions or root rots. Their growth may be decreased and yield is reduced. Some species of damping off fungi also attack fleshy organs like fruits, tubers or vegetables which show rot symptoms in the field or during storage, Adlam, (John, 2012).

Seedlings Showing Damping off of Symptoms

### Die-back

A gradual death of affected region from top to bottom takes places, such drying and death of infected host symptoms are called as Die back disease. It is caused by seed or soil borne pathogen. Most of the forest trees, fruit plants and ornamentals are susceptible for die back pathogen (Alexopoulos and Mims, 1979).

The twig and branches of infected plant dry up from the top to bottom. On the dried region, a small, black dot like acervuli of the fungus appear. Infected pods shrivel and dry up. Exm: Die back of Cowpea (*Vigna sinensis*) is caused by *Colletotrichum capsici*.

### Mould

The symptoms termed mould because of moldy growth of fungus which is responsible for deterioration of stored seeds, fruits and vegetables.

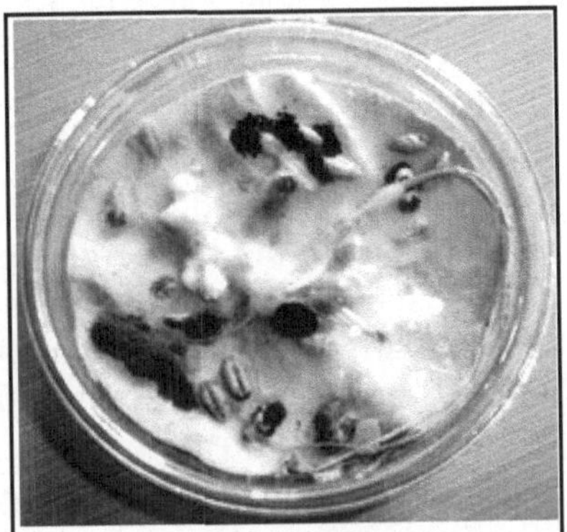

Healthy Seedlings

#### *Grain Mould*

Just before maturity the grains in the ear of *bajra* or *jowar* get infected with air borne mycoflora. The infected grains show moldy growth of fungi. The entire surface of the grains gets covered by fungal hyphae and spores. The infected grains become unfit for consumption because of moldy growth of fungus. The symptoms are termed as grain mould. A grain mould disease is very common if the food grains are stored without drying (Reed, *et.al*, 2007). The saprophytic mycoflora grow on seeds causing seed deterioration due to moldy growth of saprophytic fungi. The saprophytes produce mycotoxins which is toxic substance. The affected grains are unfit for consumption. The fungal genera causing grain mould are *Aspergillus, Fusarium. Rhizopus, Mucor, Penicillium, Curvularia, Cladosporium* etc.

### *Sooty Mould*

A dark brown to black firm or crust like growth of fungus occur on leaf as well as on leaf sheath. They grow on intact secretions of leaf. Exm: sooty mould of sugar cane is caused by *Capnodium.*

### *Black Mould*

The infected tissue becomes water soaked and a very soon entire onion bulb turn soft rotted. Infected region get covered with mycelial mat and numerous black spores. The symptoms termed as black mould due to black moldy growth of fungus. The black mould disease of onion is caused due to infection of *Aspergillus niger.*

### *Grey Mould of Cotton*

First of all grey mildew disease occurs on the leaves which are close to the soil surface. The spots are developed on leaves which are light green to yellowish in colour which measure 3-4 μm in diameter. The spots are bounded by veins hence resemble the angular leaf spot disease. The fungal growth is visible on the lower surface of infected leaf. During moist weather the spots turn whitish in colour. At maturity the lesion dry up and a patch of dead tissue (necrosis) occur. Heavy defoliation occurs in severe cases of disease development. The grey mildew disease of cotton is caused by *Ramularia areola.* It is a soil borne pathogenic fungus.

*Blue Mould*

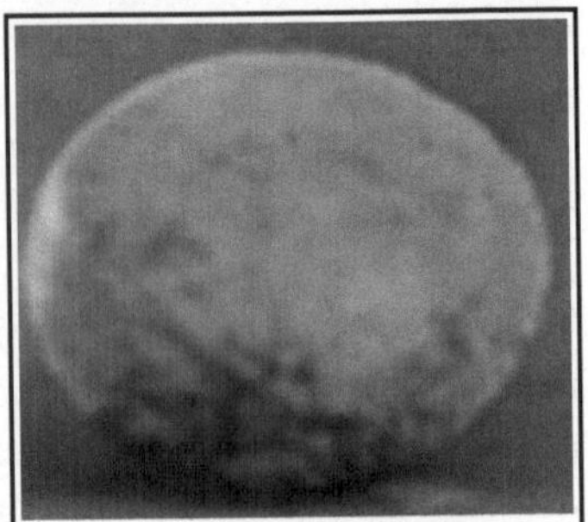

Green Mould of Amla (*Penicillium*)

The blue mould of apple is caused by *Penicillium expansum*. The infected fruit initially show a slightly depressed water soaked spot, which gradually increase in all directions, involving most of the area of fruit. The pulp of fruit turns soft and light brown in colour due to biochemical alteration. Such fruits are unfit for consumption. The rotted fruits emit mouldy odour. High humidity favours the disease. The affected region of fruit gets covered with mycelial mat and numerous fungal spores of grayish blue in colour. Entire fruit get rotted within 10 days of infection. It is a very common post-harvest disease of many types of fruits which occur during transportation and storage periods.

**Gummosis**

The symptoms are characterized by release of sticky substance from the affected plant parts. It is gum-like substance gets deposited on infected plant. The symptoms are termed as gummosis. On the basis of symptoms the disease is termed as gummosis (Arneson, 2001).

**Hypertrophy**

Hypertrophy Symptoms

Abnormal increase in size or shape due to excessive enlargement of the size of cell of a particular tissue due to infection of pathogenic organism is termed as hypertrophy. It is the outer growth of affected region caused due to fungal, bacterial and nematodal parasites. The abnormal growth of affected part disturbs the physiological and biochemical processes of plant (Drenth, 2004).

## Hydrosis

A water soaked lesions are developed on any part of plant which secret watery substance. Such symptoms are developed by a variety of biotic and abiotic factor in plants. It is a structural change occurs in affected plant part. The affected region consists of water soaked necrotic lesion.

## Leaf Spot

The mycoflora of the class Deuteromycetes causes leaf spot diseases of herbs, shrubs and trees. The fungi causing leaf spot disease enters the leaf through stomata. The fungal spores germinate on leaf surface in presence of little moisture. Some fungi produce cell wall degradation enzymes cellulose and enter the leaf. There is great variation in colour, size and shape of the spot produced by infectious fungi, (Narasimha *et.al*, 2012).

The fungi caused leaf spot diseases are numerous. In leaf spot diseases the host cells are killed in a limited area to form lesion or spot. The spots are of various sizes and shapes as zonate, target, broad, angular, or of frog eye type. The tar spots are of characteristic type of leaf spots which appear slightly raised, black in colour and a flat drop of tar on leaves. The pathogenic fungi *Rhytisma* and *Phyllachora* cause tar spot disease of plants. *Alternaria solani* produces a spot on leaves of tomato or potato which consists of concentric rings. In some cases the dead tissues shrink and drop off. The stage is known as shot hole. The leaf spots are developed when the pathogen enters the leaf tissue. The pathogenic fungus absorbs food material from the infected tissue by sending haustoria into the host cells (Bengtsson, 2006). The affected region of leaf shows spots of variable shapes, sizes and colours. The fungi responsible for leaf spots of various plants are *Cercospora, Phyllachora, Phyllosticta, Septoria, Colletotrichum, Carynespora, Chaetothyrium, Pseudocercospora, Fusarium, Myrothecium, Drechslera, Ciliochorella, Curvularia, Pseudodiploidia, Phoma, Drechslera, Mycosphaesella and Septoria.*

Tikka Disease of Groundnut

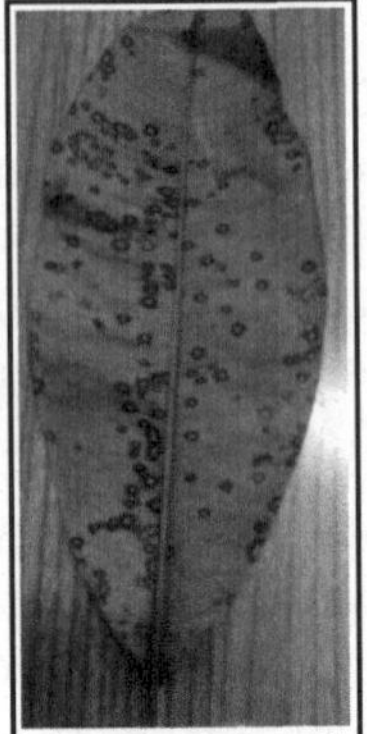

Septoria Leaf Spots

Back Leaf Spot of Rose

*Types of Leaf Spots*

*(i)* **Russet Spot:** The leafy vegetables give off ethylene after harvest which is a ripening phenomenon. Rueest spotting is caused due to production of ethylene in continuation, (Holb, 2009). The spots are more distinct on upper surface than lower surface. Russet spots are chocklet coloured.

*(ii)* **Tan Spot:** Tan spot develops initially as yellow tan flecks on both upper and lower surfaces. The spots increase into lens shaped tan blotches with yellow borders. A characteristic of tan spot is small dark brown in centre. Exm. *Pyrenophora trichostoma* causes tan spots on wheat leaf (Keitt, 1937).

*(iii)* **Floury Leaf Spot:** The lower older leaves show yellow spots which gradually progress upwards. In case of severe infection, leaves show yellow mottling and at maturity spots become brown. The brown spots encircled with yellow margins. Usually the spots are 2-3 mm in diameter; many spots get coalesce to form large patches. On the upper surface of spot, white fluty growth of pathogenic fungus and conidiophores can be seen which give to the leaf the appearance of having been sprinkled with coarse flour, hence the disease is

named as floury leaf spot. The infected leaves turns brown and shed off permanently at any stage of its growth. It affects yield of crop.

*(iv)* **Cavity Spot:** The spot may be small, spherical, or oval in shape, 1-3 mm is diameter. The spot resemble cavity. The tissues over the larger lesion tend to rupture, living a ragged fringe and the cavity is lined with mycelial threads of fungal pathogen. The spots develop during growth of plant but the cavity spots remain visible even after harvest of crop. The soil borne pathogen *Pythium violae* infects the carrot and produce cavity spots (Green & Makin, 1985).

*(v)* **Frog Eye Leaf Spot:** The infection starts as a small, spherical to somewhat irregular lesion on the upper surface of leaf. The spots are water soaked which are brown in colour and reddish brown distinct margin. At maturity the centre of spot becomes grey coloured. Many spots coalesce to form large blighted areas on leaf. Drying and defoliation are common symptoms. Such type of symptoms termed as frog eye spots. The frog eye spot disease of soybean is caused by *Cercospora sojina.*The pods also possess such type of spots.

*(vi)* **Greyish White Spot:** Grey coloured white spots are produced by *Cercospora ricinella* on castor (*Ricinus communis*) leaf. The spots are surrounded by deep brown band which may be narrow and diffused.

*(vii)* **Concentric Spot:** The concentric rings develop in the mature spot that indicate the gradual growth of respective pathogenic fungus inside the host tissue. The pathogen *Phytopthora colocaceac* causes concentric spots on Castor *(Ricinus communis)* leaf. *Alternaria solani* causes concentric rings in the spots on potato leaf.

*(viii)* **Brown Eye Spot:** Sutton and Waller, (1988) reported brown spots on leaves of coffee (*Coffea arabica* L.) due to infection of *Cercospora coffeicola* Berk & Che.

*(ix)* **Dollar Spot:** Tsai, J.N. of Taiwan found leaf spots of turf grass caused by *Sclerotinia homoeocarpa.* The spots resemble as dollar hence it is called dollar spot. The affected leaf exhibits white straw coloured lesions that increase gradually. Each spot is surrounded by brown coloured border. Infected leaves become blighted.

*(x)* **White Spot:** The pathogen produces circular whitish spots all over the host leaf lamina. Mostly the spots are encircled by reddish band. Later on it develops into brown patch. Exm: *Cylindrocladium quinquiseptatum* cause white spot on clove leaf.

*(xi)* **Oval Spot:** Harris (2008) reported occurrence of oval spots caused by *Phyllosticta gingiber* on leaves of ginger (*Zingiber officinalis*) at very initial stage of development of disease. The fully developed spots are whitish in the centre and have dark brown margin with a yellowish halo around the spot.

*(xii)* **Ink Spot:** Jacob (2009) reported ink spot disease occur on leaves of Aspen (a wood yielding tree). Initially tan to brown areas appears on the upper leaf surfaces. The spots consist of concentric, discoloured ring pattern which is visible. The affected region shows black bodies of fungus which are hard, oval and nearly 1/4 inch long. Such spots are called ink spots.

*(xiii)* **Red Spot:** Mueller and Schmit (2006) reported red spot development on the leaf of blackberry due to the infection of *Septoria rubi.*

*(xiv)* **Black Leaf Spot:** The leaflet of rose possesses black coloured spots which are encircled with yellow chlorotic hollow. The spots are distinct on both the surfaces of leaf. The spots increase in size. In severe cases, the entire leaf gets involved and fell off. Heavy defoliation affects the flower

**Back Leaf Spot of Rose**

formation. Even the pedicel and stem possesses black spot of fungus. During humid weather the spread of disease takes place very fast, Watt (2010). The black leaf spot disease of rose is caused by *Diplocarpon rosae.*

*(xv)* **Melanose Spot:** The leaf spots caused by Septoria species on black grape (*Vitis nucifera*) are called as melanose spots at Eastern and Midwestern United states of America. The spots are called melanose.

*(xvi)* **Superficial Spot:** The fungal forms causing powdery mildews of different plants produce superficial growth of mycelium on the host leaf and all other parts of plant except root system. At the initial stage of disease development, small greyish superficial spots are formed on the infected host leaf. The fungal pathogen *Erysiphe polygoni* produce superficial spots on infected plant part at initial stage of disease development, (Srivastava, 1985).

*(xvii)* **Amorphous Leaf Spot:** Takimoto (1919) reported occurrence of amorphous leaf spots on Ginseng (*Panex ginseng*) due to infection of *Colletotrichum dematium* (pers)) Grove.

*(xviii)* **Freckle Spot:** These are brown to black crustations with longitudinal cracks on fruit skin. The fruits start drying and pulp also get discoloured. Such types of symptoms occur on banana fingers due to infection of *Macrophoma musae.*

*(xix)* **Dimond Spot:** On the mature banana fingers the diamond spots are developed due to infection of *Cercospora hayi.* The spots are yellowish raised areas which measure about 5 mm in diameter. The spot dry up and turn to necrosis. The necrotic spot becomes 1.5 cm in width. Such spot are called as dimond spots which develop during transportation period.

*(xx)* **Target Spot:** The infected leaf possesses reddish brown circular or irregular spots which are variable in size from tiny dots to 1 cm in diameter. The larger spots develop as target like concentric rings. The central

regions of spot consist of dead tissue. Spot is surrounded by yellow halo. Leaves fell off before maturity. Such types of symptoms are termed as target spots.Exm: Target spot of soybean is caused by *Corynespora cassicola.*

*(xxi)* **Eye Spot:** The initial symptoms develop as a elongated pale yellow leaf spots on both the side of the young leaves. Later on at maturity the spots turn red with yellow margin. As the leaf dies its tip becomes reddish brown giving a brownish appearance to the field. Such types of symptoms are termed as eye spot. Exm: An Eye spot of sugarcane is caused by *Helminthosporium sacchari.*

*(xxii)* **Red Spot:** The red leaf spots are caused by *Septoria* in a variety of plants. The red spots symptoms consist of a lesion with grey center and brown to red coloured border. Mostly the spots are spherical about 2-4 mm in the diameter. The spots consist of black dot like fruiting bodies. The red spots of blackberry in caused by *Septoria rubi.*

*(xxiii)* **Sharp Eye Spot:** The symptoms which consist of lesions which are more distinct and very sharply cutlined than those of normal spots. The centre of mature spot consists of mycelial threads. Such types of symptoms are caused by *Pseudocercosporella herpotrichoides* in certain grasses.

### Shot Hole

In many vegetables, cereals, pulses, the infected plants shows leaf spots caused by fungal parasites like, *Cercospora, Alternaria,* and *Phyllosticta* etc. By the time the affected region of leaf drops off due to which spherical holes are formed on the leaf surface. Such symptoms are termed as shot hole. In certain leaf spot disease caused by fungal pathogens, the infected spot consists of dead tissue which is easily ejected from the spot and a hole is formed at the region of spot on the infected leaf blade. Hence the infected leaf possesses holes. This type of symptoms is termed as shot holes. The number of holes correlated with number of necrotic spots of infected leaf ejected. In certain plants the many shot holes are developed on leaf due to insect feeding. The shot hole symptoms are restricted to leaf only.

**Leaf Weathering**

Weathering of leaf may be pathogenic or non-pathogenic disorder in which gradual drying of leaf from top to bottom or bottom to top takes place. Withering of leaf of jack fruit caused by *Colletotrichum gloesporioides* initially shows dark areas on leaf which advances extending along the veins of leaf edges. The affected leaves turn brown and their margins roll upward (Rawal & Saxena, 1997). The basal rot disease of onion caused by *Fusarium oxysporum* in the field shows withering of leaf which starts from top to bottom rapidly. Batista (1947) reported weathering of young green leaves start first at the base of leaf and then extending outward along the vein in case of dieback disease of many forest plants caused by *Botryodiploidia theobromae.*

Leaf Weathering

**Leaf Drooping**

In many economically important plants there is heavy defoliation of leaves, flowers and fruits. The symptoms are termed as leaf or fruit or flower drooping. Various factors (biotic and non-biotic) responsible for drooping of leaves.

**Black Point**

All the stages of the plant growth are susceptible to the infection of the pathogen. The pathogenic fungus causes post-emergence rot disease of seedling and the leaf spot

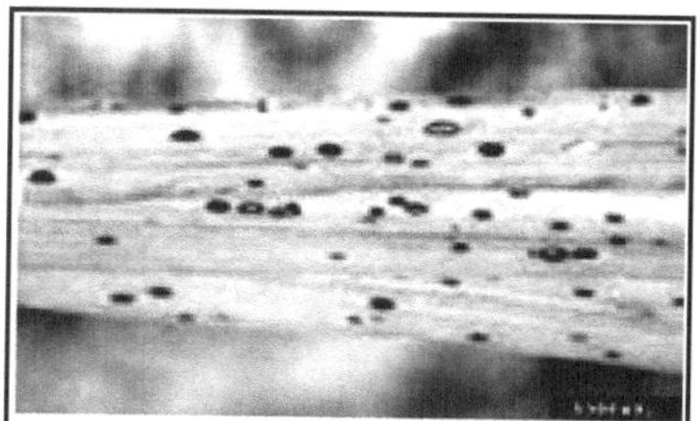

Brown Spot of Rice

disease of mature plants, (McManus *et.al*, (2005). Initially the infected seedling show yellowish oval to oblong spot mostly on the cotyledons in the form of linear streaks which later get metamorphosis into dry straw coloured patches. The infected leaves may have elongated spots. The centre of the spot is ash coloured with brownish border. There is a distinct yellow halo which is present around the spot. (Fernandez, 2011). The black point disease of wheat is caused by *Helminthosporium sativum*, King and Bakke.

### Blast

The leaves get affected heavily which may have spindled shaped spots on the upper surface. The spots vary greatly in their length from 0.5 cm to several cm. The centre of the fully developed spot turn's whitish grey. The margin of the spot is mostly dark brown. In severe cases of disease development the neck of the panicle turns dark black. Shriveling of neck occurs which is a common symptom (Blas and Calderone, 2008). The disease is caused by *Pyricularia oryzae cavara.*

### Defoliation

The leaves of infected plants fell off before maturity or at any stage of its development. The symptoms are termed as defoliation. In case of wilt diseases of a variety of plants heavy leaf fall occur due to lack of water the leaves of infected plants becomes yellowish later on the leaves get dried. Drying of leaves takes place due to blockage of vascular system of infected plant due to growth of fungal hyphae inside the water supplying vessels. Defoliation is caused by a variety of fungal pathogens (Marwa *et.al.* (2009).

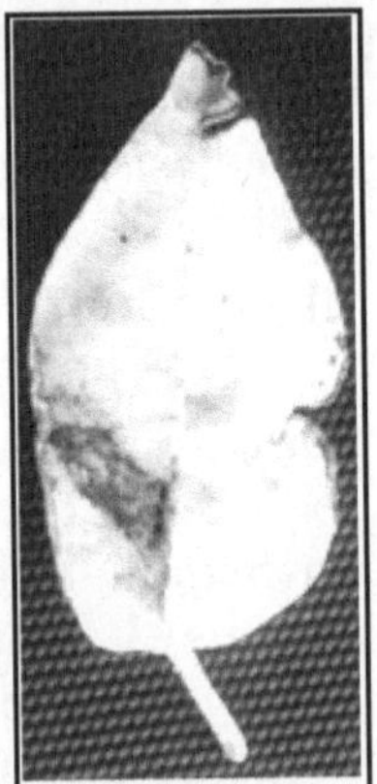

Chlorosis

### Chlorosis

The reduced functioning of chlorophyll results into a various kinds of chlorosis. The chlorosis may be due to mineral deficiency, viral disease, wilt, or any other agencies. The symptoms chlorosis is initiated due to interaction of pathogen with host cells. The normal functioning of chlorophyll in the cell get disturbed due to infection. Initially yellow spots or streaks are developed which are called as chlorotic spots. Chlorosis may takes place in the form of patches or streaks or entire leaf or whole plant sometimes shows chlorosis. It affects the rate of photosynthesis and indirectly reduces the yield of affected plant (Thakur *et.al.*, 2006).

**Necrosis**

Necrosis means large patch of dead tissues occur on leaf, stem or fruit. It is the most destructive types of effect. Such diseases are caused by pathogens like *Pythium, Botrytis,* and *Fusarium* mineral deficiency etc. It causes immediate and severe damage to the affected host tissues and obtains their nutrients from cell killed in advance. Necrosis is the symptom which consists of spots or blighted areas which consists of dead tissue. All the fungi causing leaf spots and blight diseases shows necrosis in infected host plant part. Drying and defoliation are very common after development of necrosis. Necrosis is caused by specialized parasites like *Puccinia, Phytopthora, Venturia, Taphrina, Alternaria, Colletotrichum,* or mineral deficiency etc., (Shirshikar, 2008).

**Necrosis of *Tectona grandis* leaf**

**Stripe**

The stripe symptoms are caused by a variety of plant pathogens. The symptoms include narrow, elongated spots that are arranged in parallel fashion between the veins of monocot leaf. The stripe later on turns reddish to purple in colour. The strip symptoms are the chlorotic streaks. The stripe symptoms are mostly common on infected leaf. The spots are narrow, elongated which are 3-7 mm wide with distinct margin. The spots are formed in parallel fashion between the veins of monocot leaf. Marwat *et.al.*, (2009). The stripe later on turns reddish to purple in colour. The strip symptoms are the chlorotic streaks. If they are formed before formation of cereals, it causes drying of leaves and death of immature plants.

*Red Strip*

The red strip disease observed at maturity of rice plants. The combination of high humidity and high temperature is favourable for infection. Initially a very small 1-2 mm sized spots are developed on leaves which are yellow to dark brown in colour. The lesions are elongated, which are parallel to the veins. In severe cases the spots coalesce to form large elongated red coloured stripes. The spots initiate from leaf sheath and progress upward to the tip of the leaf. Exm: The red stripe disease of rice is caused due to a bacterial pathogen defoliation is common.

**Mildews**

The mildews are the diseases in which the pathogen appears outside the host. The mildews pathogens grow mostly superficially on host surface. They appear as white, grey, brownish or purple patches, on leaves, stem or flowering of the host plant. The mildews are of three types (Glawe, 2008):

*(i)* Downy mildew;

*(ii)* Powdery mildew; and

*(iii)* Grey mildew.

*Downy Mildew*

In case of downy mildews, the pathogens occur on ventral surface of the leaf. The pathogen produces numerous sporangia which emerge through stomata present on ventral region of the leaf, which are visible. Downy mildew of pea (*Pisum sativum*) caused by *Perenospora pisi*. Downy mildew of crucifer (*Albugo candida*),

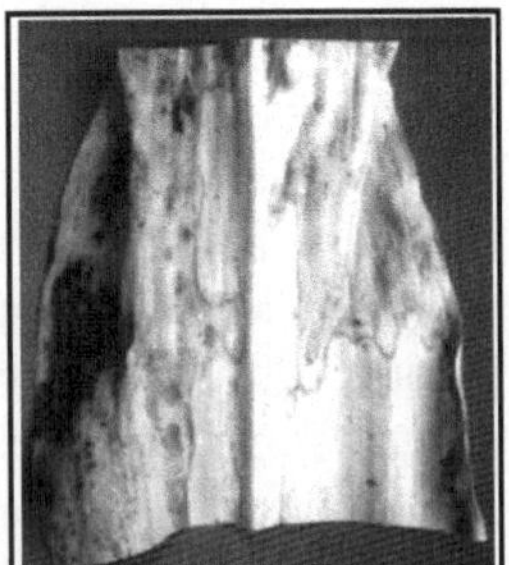

Downy Mildew of Sorghum

Downy mildew of grapes (*Plasmapara viticola*), downy mildew of bajra (*Sclerospora graminicola*), Downey mildew – Sorghum – *Peronosclerospora sorghi,* (Thakur *et.al,* 2006).

Downey Mildew of Dalbergia Sisso

*Powdery Mildew*

The powder mildews (Erysiplaceae) occurs on all part of the plant such as upper and lower surface of leaf, stem, and flowers except root system. The growth of the pathogenic fungus is superficial, white powdery in appearance. It consists of numerous conidiophores and conidia. Powdery mildew greatly reduces the yield (Munjal *et.al,* 1963). (Scarito G., 2007). Example: Powdery mildews of pea (*Erysiphe polygoni*), Powdery mildew – sesamum – *Alternaria sesame,* Powdery mildew of teak (*Tectona grandis*).

Powdery Mildew of Teak
(*Uncinulla necator*)

*Grey Mildew*

The grey mildew is observed in cotton due to infection of *Ramularia areola.* The characteristic lesions on leaves are developed. The spots are yellowish green, irregular, angular and delimited by veins. On the lower surface of lesion. There is visible growth of fungus giving whitish appearance. Defoliation is common, it causes premature opening of cotton balls.

**Proliferation**

The bajra ear gets infected by *Sclerospora graminicola* replace all the grains with a leafy structure. The entire or half of the ear show leafy structures. These symptoms are termed as proliferation (Alexopoulos and Mims, 1979).

**Pitting**

In case of pitting the infected part of plant show depressed tissue in small areas which is repeated many times.

Such types of symptoms are termed as pitting. Such a numerous depressed small areas developed due to pathogenic organism. Due to pitting the affected plant part do not shed off. He affected plant part remains attached with parental plant. When such a pitting symptoms develop on the fruits it is termed as fruit pitting. The pitting symptoms are caused by bacterial plant pathogenic organisms. The pitting symptoms are small, circular in outline, depressed and many in number. Any disease or any type of symptoms affects the yield of the plant (Pockman, *et.al.*, December 1995).

**Rot Diseases**

The saprophytic forms of fungi imperfecti enter into the injured fruits and causes rot diseases. The soft skinned fruits are more susceptible for infection of saprophytic mycoflora. The infected fruits are unfit for consumption; because of biochemical changes in the fruit pulp such fruits becomes toxic. The rot diseases of fruits which occur after harvest during storage period are termed as post-harvest diseases. Fruit rot diseases mostly occurs during transportation and storage periods. Fruit rots are mostly caused by mold fungi like *Aspergillus, Penicillium, Rhizopus, Fusarium, Colletotrichum* etc. The affected fruits loose turgidity; the infected fruit pulp get macerated and a foul smell comes out from the infected fruits. In severe cases the moldy growth of fungus appear on the affected areas (Kumari, *et.al.*, 2012).

Exm: Stem end rot of mango (*Aspergillus niger*); Rhizopus rot of papaya (*Rhizopus arrhizus*) Penicillium rot of Amla (*Penicillium islandicum*); *Phytopthora* rot of guava (*Phytopthora psidi*), etc.

**Different Types of Rot Diseases**

*Neck Rot*

Initially a water soaked spot is formed on the leaf or any part of plant just above the soil surface. The spot gradually turn to soft. The decayed region looses moisture and a sunken spot is developed.

The sunken spot get covered with dense mycelial mat and short conidiophores and conidia of the pathogen. Later on black coloured sclerotial bodies are formed. Such symptoms are observed in onion plants before harvest which is caused by *Botrytis allii.*

### *Fibrous Root Rot*

The fibrous root rot symptom of certain economically important plants is caused by soil borne pathogenic fungus *Phytopthora* sp. Initially the fungus infects the root system. The tips of main root and secondary root show dieback symptoms. The root tip gradually dies from top to bottom. Such an infected plant also shows shoot tip dies back symptoms. Leaf turn yellow, plants possesses very week branches. The roots turn dark brown which lack fibrous roots. The root tissue turns brown. Such symptoms are termed as fibrous root rot.

### *Curd Rot*

Initially a water soaked lesion is formed on the fruit or leaf or tender part of infected plant. The spot increase rapidly. The tissue turns to brown in colour which emits foul smell within short period after infection. It causes standing wilting and death and decay of plant. The symptoms are termed as curd rot. The curd rot disease of cabbage heads is caused by bacterial pathogen *Erwina carotovora.*

### *Bud Rot*

The bud rot of coconut in commonly observed in India. It is caused by *Phytopthora palmivora.* The fungus attack at any stage of plant development. The leaves at the growing region are very young which turn yellowish. Such infected leaf can be easily removed. The infection spread on other mature leaves in the form of many sunken spots. The spots are irregular in shape and size. The growing points turn brown and dry up. Such symptoms are termed as bud rot.

### *Pink Rot*

In the mature crop of potato, the pink rot appears which causes stunting of plant, yellowing of leaves, defoliation, and discolouration of vascular tissue. The roots turn brown to dark black in colour. Sometimes aerial tubers develop. Decay of tubers start near stolon end region of tuber. The affected tissue of tuber turns corky. When the infected tubers cut open, it consists of cream to pink coloured tissue which is delimited by dark brownish margin. Later on the affected tissue becomes soft. When the infected potatoes cut open and exposed to air, that gradually turn pinkish, within few minutes. The pink rot of potato in caused by a soil or seed borne fungus called as *Phytopthora erythroseptica.*

### *Wet Rot*

The parts of chilly plant get infected with infections fungus *Choanephora cucurbitarum* produces wet rot symptoms. The infection is especially occur on flower buds as well as mature flowers, leaves, young fruits. The infected part show turns dark green, soft and wet. In case of severe disease development, the rotted region gets covered with interwoven mycelia mat with black dot like sporangia. The wet rot of chilly is caused by *Choanephora cucurbitarum.*

### *Sour Rot*

The characteristics symptoms of sour rot symptoms are development of water soaked regions especially at the region of cracks on the tomato fruits. The water soaked region appears dull. From such region, decay extends to other healthy part of fruit. There is great alteration of food content of tomato. A typical sour odour is emitted from such infected tomatoes. Such fruit s gets rotted during transportation and storage periods. Such type of signs caused due to fungal pathogen termed as sour rot. The responsible pathogen casing sour rot of tomatoes is *Geotrichum candidum.*

### *Dry Rot*

The infected tuber showing dry rot symptoms include grey to black coloured sunken spots on the infected tubers. The tubers dry up fade up, show shriveling, and a whitish growth of entophytic fungus becomes visible in the farm of thin mycelia smut on affected region of tubers (Babu, 2010).

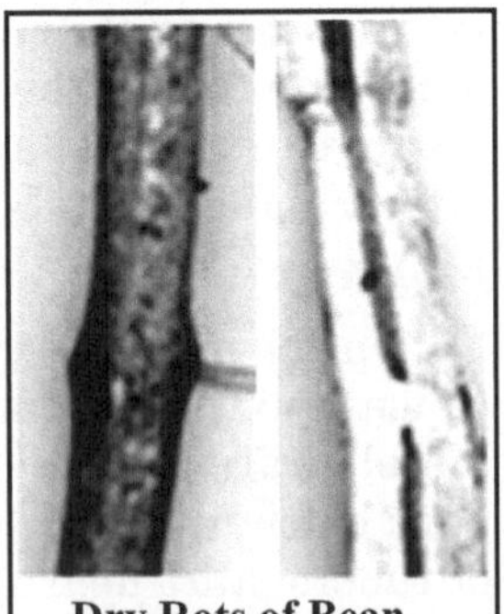

**Dry Rots of Bean**

At low temperature during storage, such tubers become hard and firm. The disease is caused by soil or seed borne pathogenic fungus *Fusarium sp.* Dry root rot of cotton (*Macrophomina phaseolina*).

*Root Rot*

Root Rot of Cotton

The disease causes sudden wilting of entire plant. The disease spread in the crop field in the form of concentric circles. Infected plants may have rotted root system. In severely infected plants the tap root remains attached to the plant and remaining root system get decayed that remain in field soil. The woody part of the plant turns black on which black dot like sclerotia occur. The transverse section of the infected root shows brown tissue due to presence of intracellular hyphal threads (Cook, Allyn-Austin, 1981). All the stages of plant growth are susceptible for infection of the pathogen. The soil borne pathogen attacks the radical of seedling; later on the cotyledons of seedling get attacked by pathogen. Gradually seedling becomes yellow and dry up. The adult plant when get infected; the infection occur at root system. The infected root system show rotting of root. The root hairs get killed and shed off. The outermost layer of rotted root turns black, rough because of occurrence of many dots like sclerotia. Sclerotia are the fruiting body like structures which consists of numerous fungal threads along with spores. The stem of infected plant remains straight; there are no water soaked spots on stem of infected plant. In the field the disease spread in the form of ring. This is the distinguished characters of the disease from damping off disease.

If the infected plants are pulled out, it may have completely rotted root system. The thinner roots completely vanished the tap root remain intact for sometime but in severe cases of disease development the tap-root get detached from the plant due to excess of rot system. The parenchymatous tissue of tap root show necrosis, turn black and destroyed. The root rot of cotton is also known as dry root rot disease.

*Collar Rot*

Collar rot of papaya the disease initially appears in the form of water soaked spots on stem just above the soil surface. The spots gradually increase in size around the stem. The affected parts start rotting due to interaction of pathogen, which turn dark brown to black in colour. Rotting of girdle region of stem disturb the water supply for some extent hence, the leaves turn yellowish due to disfunctioning of chlorophyll. Defoliation of premature leaves occur which affect the total yield of plant.

*Bitter Rot*

The infection occurs at the region of peduncles of unripe berries. The affected berries droop off before maturity. Sometimes the entire bunch of berried get destroyed by the fungus. The affected berries do not get shrivel but that turn to dark brown. The brown circular spots are developed on the skin of the affected berries. In severe cases acervuli are produced on the affected region. The bark of the stems shows longitudinal cracks. The weathering of leaves is common. *Greeneria fuliginea* causes bitter rot symptoms of grapes (Fatima *et.al.*, 2006).

**Bitter Rot of Grapes**

*Soft Rot*

At the initial stage of infection the infected berries show slightly depressed spots which later turn dark brown in colour. The spots increase in size and get covered by hyaline to pink coloured threads of fungal hyphae. In severe cases of disease development the pathogenic fungus produce numerous fruiting bodies that are spread over the affected region of the berries. Soft rot disease of grapes is caused by *Periconia sarasvatipurensis.* The soft rot of banana (*Fusarium roseum*); Soft rot of apple (*Rhizopus orrhizus*).

*Red Rot*

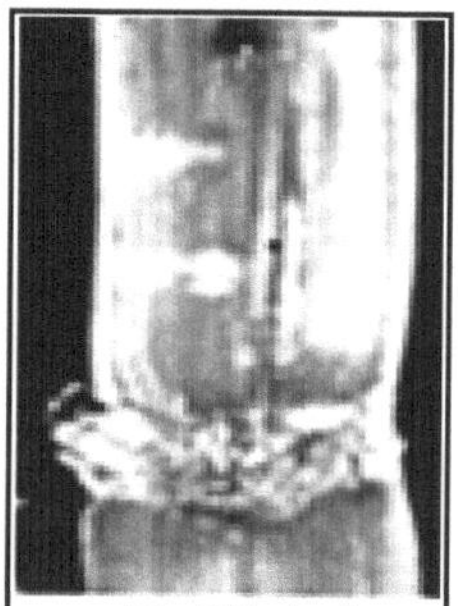

Red Rot of Sugarcane

The infected plants show stunted growth. The mid rib of the leaf possesses dark red elongated lesion which are with dark margin. The centre of the lesion turns straw coloured due to powdery growth of the respective fungus. The split open canes show red coloured vascular tissue and pith which is interrupted with white bands. There are many acervuli that are randomly distributed on the affected region of the plant (Khan, 2007); (Babu, 2010). Split open sett shows red colour of the pith which is interrupted by white bands. Red coloured of the pith is formed due to the interaction of host and pathogen (Dhingra and Sinclair, 1978). The red rot disease of sugarcane is caused by *Colletotrichum falcatum* Went.

*Stylar End Rot*

The stylar end rot symptoms of guava are caused by *Gloeosporium psidii*. Initially a discoloured region is developed near the mother end point of guava fruit. The discoloured spot increase gradually in all direction. The older spot turn brown and the pulp of fruit becomes soft. Infected fruits get shrinked; a ring of wrinkles develop on the infected fruits. Dark black pycnidia develop on entire region of affected fruit. Such symptoms are termed as stylar end rot.

*Basal Rot*

It is a very common disease of vegetables. The symptoms appear as wilting and rapid drying back of leaves from tip of the plant near maturity. The infected stem show brown discolouration. The basal rot disease of onion is caused by *Fusarium oxysporum*. The infected onion plant showing wilting and rapid dying back of leaves from tip of the top to bottom. The stem just above soil surface star rotting. Stem tissue turns to brown. Such bulb cannot be stored for longer duration. The symptoms termed as basal root, and the disease is also termed as basal rot. The basal rot of onion is caused due to fungal pathogen (*Fusarium oxysporum*), it is a soil borne pathogen. The basal rot of several vegetables is caused by *Fusarium oxysporum.*

*Foot Rot*

It is a soil borne disease. All the stage of plant growth is susceptible for infection. When the seedling gets infected, it may die or fail to emerge or grow into a delicate, unhealthy plant. The infected seedling becomes yellow, stem remains thin and tall. Within a short period the infected seedlings dry up and fell off, (Ramezani, *et.al.*, 2007). The infected adult plant show withered root system. The panicles develop or do not develop; sometimes plant produces sterile ears. The infected plant appears slightly longer than normal ones. Another important abnormality observed is that there is development of adventitious roots from lower-most nodal regions. The adventitious roots may be enveloped by leaf sheath. The split open culms show dark red colouration of the nodal region. The intermodal hollow region of stem show disposition of branched mycelium and spores (Bellaloui *et.al.*, 2008). The nodes get rotted; Culms break off easily. The affected plant dies within few days. The foot rot disease of rice is caused by *Fusarium moniliforme* Sheldom.

*Buckeye Rot*

The buck eye rot disease is firstly observed at Himachal Pradesh (Sohi, 1978). Water soaked light brown spot occur on immature tomato fruits. The spot increase in all direction, showing concentric rings which resemble the marking on the buck eye nut. The spot is dark brown and feels soft in touch. The buck eye rot of tomato is caused by *Phytopthora nicotianae.*

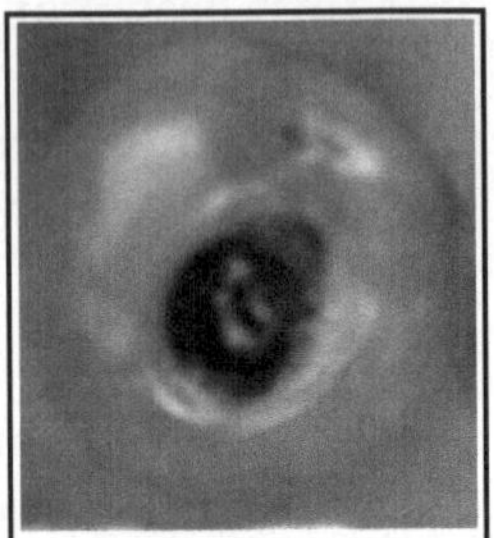

Buckeye Rot of Tomato

*Stalk Rot*

The infected stalk show dark brown to black spots that gradually girdling whole of the stem near soil surface. The stalk rot progresses deep into the stem. The pith regions of the stem get infected. The pith rot increases and a large cavity is formed which is lined with mycelium and sclerotia of the fungus. The stalk rot of certain vegetables is caused by *Sclerotinia sclerotiorum.*

*White Rot*

The seedling stage or adult stage of pea plant show white rot symptoms due to infection of sol borne fungus *Sclerotinia sclerotiorum.* The symptoms develop on any part of the plant. The infected region gets covered with white mycelial growth of fungus. Rotting of the flesh takes place. The affected region becomes white. The white rot of Seedling rots of pea is caused by *Sclerotinia sclerotiorum.*

*Seed Rot*

Ali and Dennis (1992) reported seed rot disease of coriander due to endophytic seed fungus such as *Alternaria* or *Curvularia* or *Cladospermum.* The seed get rotted at the time of germination. Such seeds do not germinate. The disease can be recognized by poor germination and stand of the crop. The seeds rot due to attack of fungi. The seedling also rot and die resulting in poor unhealthy occurrence of plants.

*Black Rot*

The affected tap root system of bean becomes rough and turns charcoal black in colour due to interaction of pathogen with host tissue. The black colour may extend slightly above the surface of the soil. At the time of high humidity and cool environment frosty growth of hyphae covers the affected area. Lateral roots get decayed and destroyed. The infected plant remains stunted and drooping of leaves occurs. The black root rot disease of bean is caused by *Thielavia basicola* (Arias, *et.al.*, 2011). The black rot of peach is caused by *Manilinia fructicola*; Black rot of pineapple is caused by *Ceatocystis paradoxa.*

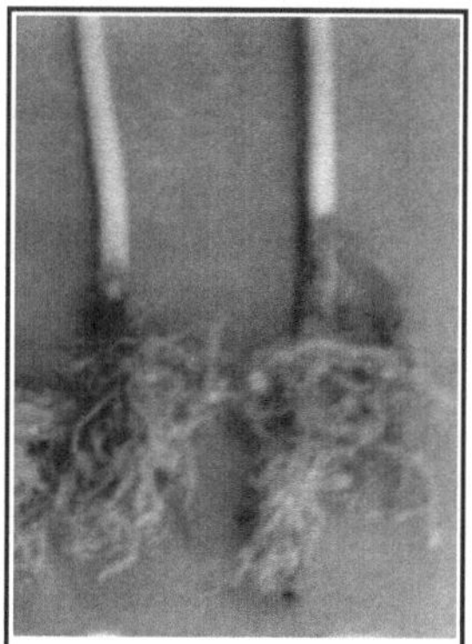

**Black Root Rot of Bean**

*Cigar End Rot*

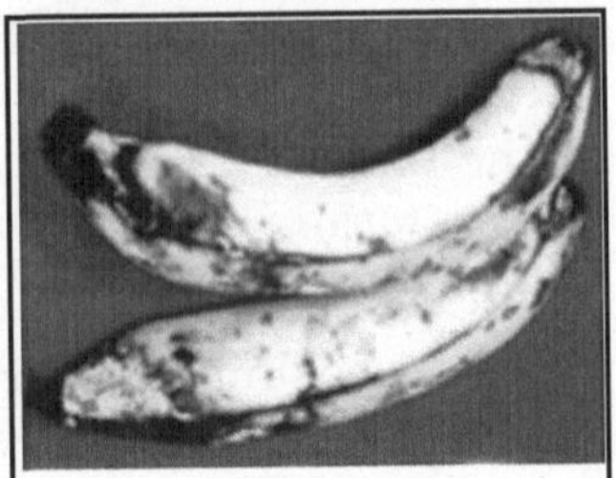

Cigar End Rot
Disease of Banana

The young fruits show infection at the end of the fruit and infected banana fingers resembles the burning cigarette. The infection proceeds from the stylar end to the bottom of the fruit. The affected region turns grey due to Sporulation of the pathogenic fungus. The affected parts get dried. In advanced stage of disease development numerous fruiting bodies appear in the infected area of the banana fingers. The ill banana fingers ripe before maturity. The disease is caused by *Stachylidium thiobromae.*

*Fruit Rot*

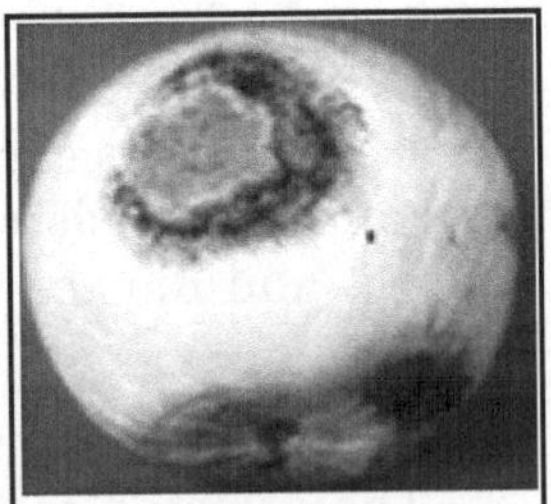

Fruit Rot

Fruit rot diseases mostly occurs during transportation and storage periods. Fruit rots are mostly caused by mould fungi like *Aspergillus, penicillium, Rhizopus, Fusarium, Colletotrichum* etc. The affected fruits loose turgidity; the infected fruit pulp get macerated and a foul smell comes out from the infected fruits. In severe cases the moldy growth of fungus appear on the affected areas.

Exm: Stem end rot of mango (*Aspergillus niger*); Rhizopus rot of papaya (*Rhizopus stolonifer*); Penicillium rot of Amla (*Penicillium* islandicum); Bacterial rot of onion (*Erwinia carotovora* sp. *carotovora*); Phytopthora rot of guava (*Phytopthora citricola*), etc.

*Stump Rot*

The stump rot symptoms are observed in lily plant due to infection of *Phytopthora nicotianae.* A typical water soaked areas develop at the base of the leaves soon after the emergence of the shoot through soil. This may result killing of entire shoot. The flower bud and tips of shoot get infected.

### *Whiskers Rot*

The symptoms mostly occur on fruits. The affected fruit show brown discoloration of the skin which peels away easily. Tissue becomes soft and watery pulp becomes sour, no smell. The entire fruit get rotted and get covered by network of fungal hyphae and numerous black fruiting bodies. The whiskers rot of apple is caused by *Rhizopus arrhizus.*

### *Stolon Rot*

Yellowing of leaves and stunting of plant occur in infected plants. In severe cases wilting of plant or the entire plant gets dried from the ground. The stolon regions get rotted. The disease becomes severe during rainy season. The stolon root disease of mint is caused due to *Macrophomina phaseoli.*

### *Sett Rots*

Set rot symptoms observed in sugar cane due to infection of *Ceratocystis paradoxa.* The exposed ends of sugarcane cuttings turn reddish and remains firm temporarily before parenchymatous tissue completely disintegrate. The internodes become hollow and black in colour. The vascular bundles remain intact. Such setts do not germinate and do not produce shoots.

### Tumefaction

The infected plant does not produce more branches but it get enlarged or elongated or distorted. Such types of symptoms are termed as tumefaction.

### Shoestrings

The infected plant possesses abnormal leaflets. The tip of leaflet gets elongated in to a long thread like structure. The greatly elongated tips of leaflet resemble the tendrils of plants but do perform the function of tendril.

### Puckering

The infected plant part get slightly raised or roughened. The surface of leaf gets broadly puckered. The symptom of such type of characteristics is termed as puckering.

### Russet

The infected fruit or any other part of plant show rough, corky patched which are uniform and thin. It may be in the form of streaks or net. Such type of features of infection is termed as russet.

### Callus

It is the outgrowth of injured region. It is developed due to healing property of meristematic tissue. Callus is a raised area which consists of bulk of meristematic tissue.

### Malformation

The infected plant produces abnormal flowers and leaves which are called as malformed flowers or leaves. Such an abnormal development of flowers or leaves is introduced by pathogenic fungus. The flowering twigs initially become multi-branched and produce large sized abnormal flowers which do not develop fruits. The growing regions of plant produce abnormal weak shoots.

### Dwarfing or Stunting

Because of infection of biotic pathogens, the infected plant do not grow properly it remains short such plant do not produce flower or fruit or produce few flower and small fruits. Because of very short size such a abnormal small plant with restricted growth in termed as stunted or dwarf plant. Such type of symptoms term as dwarfing or stunting.

### Gigantism

The part of abnormal plant show abnormal large size, due the interaction of pathogen, it is termed as gigantism.

### Rust

The members of uredinales cause rust disease in plants. The rust symptoms appear as a small pustule of spores on lower or upper leaf surface or stems of host plants. The rust pustules may be brown, black, and red, yellow or dark brown in colour that depends on the fungal genus and interaction with the host plant. The pustules are necked which break down the epidermis of host and get exposed. The list of fungi causing rust of different plants is as follow.

Rust Symptoms

Initially the mycelium of the pathogen remains in between the host cells (intercellular) and absorbs food material by sending branched haustoria into the host cells. Later on the mycelium enters the cells by rupturing cell wall. Externally the infected leaf or stem shows small pustules (Sori: group of spores) on lowers surface of infected leaf. The pustules resemble the rusty pustules which develop on iron in rainy season. Hence the disease is termed as rust disease (Mohanan, 2010). The rust is variously named. Mostly on the basis of colour of rust pustules these are named as white rust, black rust, yellow rust, brown rust etc. The mycoflora causing rust disease of plants are *Uromyces, Melampsora, Puccinia, Gymnos-porangium, Albugo, Phragmidium* etc. (Marsalis & Goldberg, 2006).

**Rust diseases of plants**

*(i)* Wheat rust: *Puccinia graminis.*

*(ii)* Rust of Coffea: *Hemileia vestatrix* (Zhang, et. al, 2012).

White Rust of Mustard

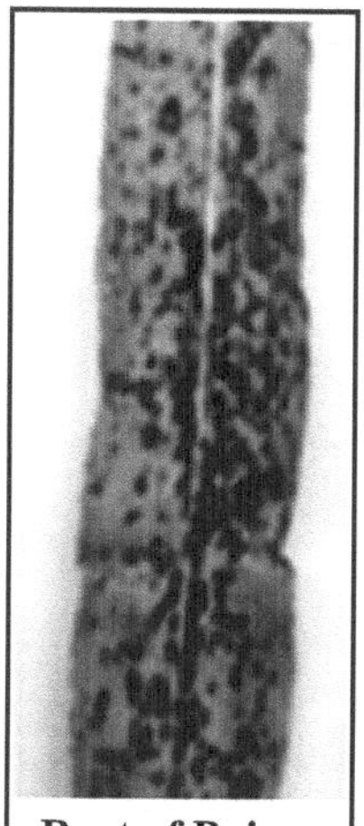
Rust of Bajra

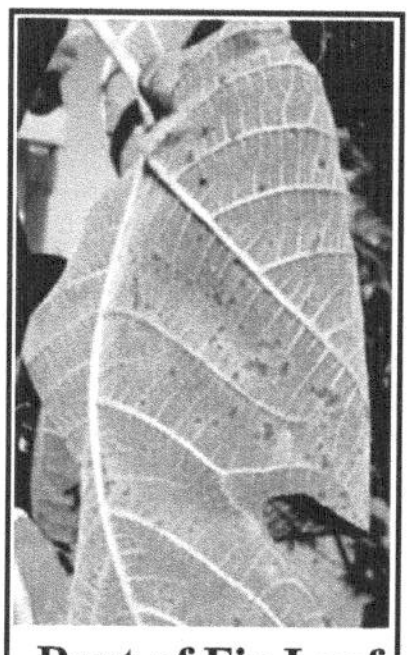
Rust of Fig Leaf

*(iii)* Rust of grapes: *Phacospora cronartiiformis*
*(iv)* Rust of fig: *Cerotelium pisi*
*(v)* Rust of asparagus: *Puccinia asparagi*
*(vi)* Rust of sunflower: *Puccinia helianthi*

Type of rust on the basis of colour of pustule:

*(i)* **Orange rust** – wheat – *Puccinia recondita*
*(ii)* **Stripe rust** – wheat – *Puccinia striformis*
*(iii)* **White rust** – mustard – Albugo *candida*
*(iv)* **Black rust** – wheat – *Puccinia graminis*
*(v)* **Yellow rust – bajra** – *Puccinia penniseti*
*(vi)* **Brown rust – wheat** – *Puccinia recondita* f.sp. *tritici*

*Yellow Rust*

The infected leaf of *bajra* show several orange – Yellow coloured minute slightly raised pustules. The uredial and telial stages of pathogen occur on *bajra* leaf. The secondary host of pathogen (*Puccinia penniseti*) is brinjal. The pycnidial and aecial stages develop on brinjal. The uredial stage on bajra leaf represented by numerous slightly raised pustules (sorus). Each pustule consists of cluster of brown uredospores (Schumann & D'Arcy, 2010). There is a small stalk supported to uredospores. The head region of uredospore protected by two layered cell wall. The inner wall is smooth and outer wall in rough and spiney. The teletospores occur on leaf sheath as well as on stem in the form of blackish teletosori. Teletosoria are rectangular in shape that consists of cluster of bicellular teletospores. The rust pustules occur on both surface of bajra leaf. Initially infection is seen on only upper half portions of leaf. All the stages of leaf growth susceptible for infection. Gradually the infected leaf dries up. It affects the yield of crop. Rust disease of bajra is caused by *Puccinia penniseti* Zimm.

*Black Stem Rust*

The rust appears in the form of elongated reddish-brown pustules (uredinia), primarily on the leaves, followed by leaf sheath and stem. Thus stem is more severely attacked (stem rust). The uredinia frequently merge with each other, and soon bursts exposing the brown powder ofurediniopores. Another kind of pustules (telia) develops later in the same sorus or independently. Telitosori are darker and by this time pustules change from brown to black in colour. These are also most prominent on culms, followed by leaf sheaths. A number of physiological changes are brought about by rust infection. The infected plants fail to produce normal ears. The grains are shriveled and lighter in weight. An increase in respiration rate accompanies infection of plant tissues by rust pathogens (Hodson, 2012) The rate of photosynthesis shows an initial increase in the entry stages of infection then is transitory and goes down finally. The causal organism of black stem rust disease of wheat is *Puccinia graminis* f. sp. *tritici.*

*Strip Rust*

The uredosori occur on lower surface of leaf. In case of severe infection affected plant show pustules on leaf sheath, stalk and glumes. Due to infection long chlorotic streaks are formed on the leaf, on which uredosori are arranged. The uredosori or pustules are fresh lemon yellow coloured (Jin, *et.al.*, 2010). The fully mature uredosori rupture the epidermis due to its growing pressure and shed off uredospores. The teletosori occur late in the season which are sub epidermal; The teletosori are black in colour somewhat rectangular in shape (Chen, 2005; de Vallavieille-Pope, *et.al.*, 2012). The stripe rust disease of wheat is caused by *Puccinia striformis* f. sp. *tritici.*

**Stripe Rust of Wheat**

*Brown Rust*

The rust pustules (uredosori) occur on leaf and leaf sheath. The pustules are randomly scattered on undersurface of leaf. The fertile mycelial mat produce cluster of uredo-spores. The growing pressure of uredospores.The the repute the epidermis. The brown coloured uredospores. The get exposed. The random distribution of uredosori and yellow colour are the distinguishing features of brown rust disease of wheat (Singh, 2008; Stone, 2010). The brown rust disease of wheat is caused by *Puccinia recondita* f.sp. *tritici*

*Orange Rust*

The symptoms of pathogen visible on lower surface of leaf in the form of orange coloured pustules which are irregularly increased and many pustules coalesce to form large affected regions. The disease symptoms are restricted to leaf only. Very rarely the shoots get infected. The photosynthetic area reduced which directly affect the yield of plant. The pustules are hypophyllous, crowdedly appeared. Gradually the coalesced pustule may have 3-25 mm in diameter. The leaves of all the age group are susceptible for infection. Infected leaves become necrotic, dry up but tend to remain attached to the infected plant. Premature drying may occur due to severe infection of the leaves. Exm: orange rust of coffee caused by *Hemileia vestatrix*.

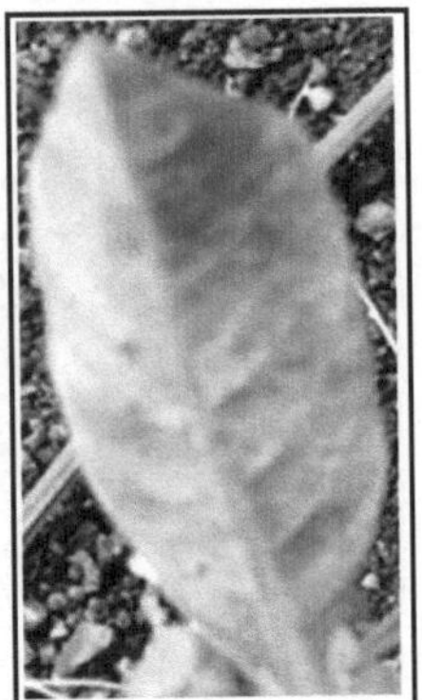

**Rust of Coffee**

*White Rust*

At the initial stage, the affected leaf shows small chlorotic spots which are randomly scattered on the leaf. At maturity, at the region of chlorotic spots small, glossy white pustules are produced in concentric ring. The pustules are visible on lower surface of leaf. The rust pustules coalesce and cover up most of the region of leaf. On fully mature rusty lesion, dark coloured oospores are produced which gives grainy appearance. The infected leaf dry up and fell off. The disease affects the total field of crops to a great extent. The white rust of crucifer is caused by *Albugo candida*.

**Resinosis**

When the infected part of plant streams resin like substance, such type of symptom is termed as resinosis.

**Smuts**

The pathogenic mycoflora of the fungal order ustilaginales infect the ovary. The infected ovaries get replaced by a compact mass of mycelial thread and spores which appear like a charcoal powder. Such diseases are termed as smuts diseases of plants. Humid environment is highly suitable for maximum development of smut diseases in the field crop (Patak and Snetselaar, 2006). The smut diseases are subdivided into different types on the basis of their appearance. The examples of smut diseases of plants are as follows:

*(i)* Loose smut of wheat – *Ustilago segetum*
*(ii)* Stinking smut – wheat – *Tilletia caries*
*(iii)* Whip smut – sugarcane – *Ustilago scitaminae*
*(iv)* Flag smut of wheat – *Urocystis tritici*
*(v)* False smut of rice – *Ustilaginoidea virens*
*(vi)* Long smut of sorghum – *Tolyposporium erhenbergii*
*(vii)* Grain smut of jowar – *Sphacelotheca sorghii*
*(viii)* Head smut of maize – *Sphacelotheca reiliana*
*(ix)* Covered smut of Barley – *Ustilago hordei*

The genera causing smut diseases of plants are *Claviceps, Sphacelotheca, Tilletia, Ustilago, Urocystis, Tolyposporium, Sporisporium* etc.

*Flag Smut*

The infected plants becomes stunted. The stunting is variable that depends on intensity of disease. Infected host plant shows excessive tillering, due to which there is no formation of ear because of no emergence of ear, it affect the yield. The leaf petiole and blade show dark grey to black coloured streaks which affect the photosynthetic process of plants. The black streak at maturity possesses black coloured smut spores intermixed with mycelial mat. The infected leaf turns sooty. Example: the wheat and many plants of graminaceae are the host of *Urocystis agropyri* which causes flag smut disease (Padmanabhan, *et.al.*, 1988).

*Whip Smut*

The entire inflorescence of infected plant gets modified into a whip like structure due to replacement of ovaries by the pathogenic fungus. Initially the whip like structure is bounded by thin silvery membrane which burst open and release spores. A very thin bright silvery membrane is present on the entire whip like inflorescence. The silvery membrane gets ruptured and release of abundance of spore balls takes place at maturity of smut spores (de Armas, *et.al.*, 2007).

**Whip Smut of Sugarcane**

The whip smut disease of sugarcane is caused by *Ustilago scitaminae*

*Covered Smut*

There are no symptoms seen on the infected plant before emergence of ear. The diseased ears are dark black smuts which emerge at the same time as the normal ears emerge in the field. Sometimes the diseased ears fail to emerge. The infected spikelet's in the ear get converted into smut sorus.

Smut sorus consists of compactly arranged teliospores. The sori get covered with ovary wall which remain intact. The smutted ears looks more distinct at maturity, which are easily recognizable in the fields (Willits and Sherwood, 1999). The smut sori, are broken only after harvest during grain removal process by mushiness or by any mechanical agency. During this process the healthy seeds get contaminated with pathogenic fungus causing covered smut disease. The pathogenic fungus is responsible for covered smut of barley is *Ustilago hordei.*

*Stinking Smut*

The infected ear of wheat shows stinking smut symptoms. The affected seed consist of smut balls (mycelium & spores). It is also known as bunt disease. Infected ears remain short. The stinking smut of wheat is caused by *Tilletia tritici.*

*False Smut*

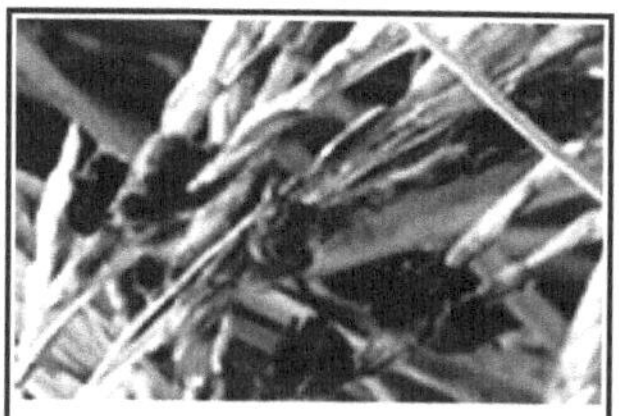

**False Smut of Rice**

The diseased plants can be identified after the formation of ear. The ovaries get utilized by the pathogen and instead of ovary small velvety green balls of the spores are developed which are slightly larger than the normal grain. The young balls are smooth and light yellow in colour which is enclosed in a thin membranous layer. The mature balls are dark brown to black in colour. The fungal hyphae occur around the glumes of the infected grain. In an ear only few of the grains show infection. The green smut or false smut disease of rice is caused by *Ustilaginoidea virens* (Cke.)

*Head Smut*

The symptoms of the disease expressed by the plant after emergence of ear. All the ovaries of flowers in the ear get transformed into a single large source. The entire sorus is covered with a silvery membrane which is delicate and white silver coloured. Later on the membrane gets ruptured by exposing numerous spore balls and mycelial threads. The exposed sorus appears dark black in colour. The spores from the head smut are easily spread or carried by wind. The head smut disease is caused by the pathogenic fungus *Sphacelotheca reiliana* (syn.)

*Loose Smut*

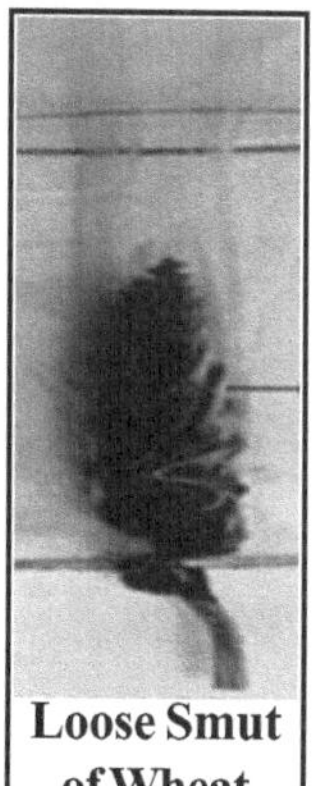

**Loose Smut of Wheat**

All the grains in the ear get replaced by abundance of mycelium and spores which shade off easily. In a bulk spore mass appear as black powdery balls. The spore masses are initially enveloped by a thin membrane which gets broken during emergence of ear. The infected ears emerge out a little before than the healthy ones. The spores are produced abundantly on the affected regions. The spores in the young spikelet's are covered by a silvery membrane (Sharifnabi, 2003 a). Pathogen responsible for loose smut disease of wheat is *Ustilago nuda.*

*Long Smut*

The long smut disease is evident due to keen observation of the ear because very few grains show infection in the ear. The ovaries of few grains replaced by smut sori. The sori are more or less elongated, longer than grain, carbon black in colour. Sori measure up to 4.0 cm in length and 0.5-1.00 cm in width. The wall of sorus made up of compactly arranged interwoven hyphae (Patel, *et.al.*, 1949). The ends of sorus are tapered; Sorus enclosed numerous spore masses. This is the disease of minor importance. The long smut disease of Sorghum is caused by *Tolyposporium ehrenbergii* (Kuhn).

**Loose Smut of Sorghum**

*Grain Smut*

The smut pathogen attack especially to the ovaries. The infected ovaries get converted into smut sori. Most of the grains in the ear get converted into sori. The grain are replaced by oval, cylindrical, grey sac like structure which are 5-15 µm in length and 3-5 µm in breadth in size. The sac is surrounded by the glumes at the base. Inside the sorus there is a mixture of hyphal threads and numerous smut spores which resemble dark black powder.

**Grain Smut of Sorghum**

In some verities the smutted grains are not much different from those of the normal. Each sorus is cylindrical, curved structure. At the centre of sorus there is column of hard tissues called collumella. The collumella is composed of the host tissues and sometimes branched at the tip. All around the collumella there is a black powdery mass of teletospores. These are hollow depressions at the surface of collumella and these are also full of spores; the sterile cells are often found mixed with the teletospores.

## Green Ear

Grain Ear of Bajra

The disease is also known as downey mildew disease of bajra. All the phases of plant growth are susceptible for disease. The infected seedlings show downey symptoms on its vegetative parts especially on growing young leaves. The typical symptoms of downey mildew can be observed after emergence of ear. The infected plant show yellowish colour of leaves, and faded thin stem. The infected ear show complete malformation of grains into leafy structures or some part of ear show grain malformation into green leafy structures. The leafy structures (modified grain) roll up or get twisted. The infected plant show stunting. Stunting and yellowing is also observed in infected seedling. The seedling turns and rolls down and dry up. Some infected plant become bushy. Leaves of infected plant show chlorotic streaks which are more distinct on upper surface of leaf. Just below the streaks on the lower surface of leaf, a profuse growth of pathogenic fungus is visible. All the affected parts of the plant becomes grayish white due to downey growth of the pathogen. The chlorotic streaks gradually turn to brown to dark brown (necrosis). The leaves dry up. In case of seedling infection, the seedling fails to develop into adult plant due to downey growth of pathogen it becomes yellowish and delicate. The seedlings dry up within a week of infection. The seedling appear whitish due to mycelium growth on its surface. The very different unexpected typical symptoms are develop on the inflorescence. Ear infection due to pathogenic fungus show transformation of ovary into green chlorophyllous leafy structure. This is the green ear phase of pathogen. This is the result of systemic infection. Different forms of infection observed in the ear. Some of the infected ears possess normal grain on half of the length of ear and remaining half portion consists of small leafy structure (ovary modified to leaf like structure). The plant in originally unbranched but due to infection, the nodal buds get activated and two or more than two branches arise from the nodal bud, so the plant appear bushy. The development of lateral shoots on nodal region indicates that the plant is infected by the pathogen *Sclerospora graminicola*. Different types of abnormalities are observed in the infected ear of bajra (Santiago *et.al.*, 2008). Ear head looks abnormal in which all the ovaries replaced by green leafy structure. In some cases the length of ear is not affected but all the ovaries of ear transformed into leafy structures. In some cases, the lower half portion of ear the ovaries modified to leafy structures and upper half of the ear consist of normal grains. In other the ovaries of middle region of ear transformed to leafy structures and upper and lower portion of ear show normal grains. The bristles of spikelet show gall like hypertrophy; at the place of one spikelet, two are formed, on the same pedicel. The stamens modified to leaf like structures. Filaments get elongated. Whole stamen gets converted into leaf like structure, which appear brownish in colour. The central region of the floret is usually elongated into leafy shoot which consist of twisted and malformed foliose leaves. There is rare development of pistil. Even pistil is replaced by leaf like structure. The green ear disease of bajra is caused by the fungal pathogen called as *Sclerospora graminicola.*

### Ergot

The pathogen replaces the grains with sclerotia or ergot body. The infected grains ooze out a sticky sweet substance contains numerous conidia of the pathogen; this is the honey dew stage of the ergot symptoms. Initially the honey dew is cream coloured, later it turn pink or brown. The duration of honey dew phase remains for about 4-7 days. After honey dew stage, with a short period of 8-10 days visible sclerotia develop at the place of grain. The ergot bodies or sclerotia are slightly larger than the normal grains. They can be seen projecting from or between the glumes. Sclerotia which are initially whitish, elongated structures which later becomes hard and brown to dark brown in colour. In some cases sclerotia do not develop and florets have a blasted appearance. Such florets remain sterile. The causal organism of ergot disease of bajra is *Claviceps fusiform.* Que *et.al.*, (2008).

**Ergot of Bajra**

### Smudge

The characteristics features of smudge are development of small dark green to black dots on the affected host. Many dots get mixed to form blotches or concentric rings. Such type of symptoms termed as smudge (Farr & Rossman, 2012). The concentric rings consist of clusters of fungal acervuli. Exm: Onion smudge caused by *Colletotrichum circinans.*

### Scab

In case of scab diseases, a rough crust like spots is formed on the affected plant part. Exm: Apple scab caused by *Venturia inaquilis.* The scab symptoms are, mostly developed on fruits and certain vegetables. The affected leaf may have black sunken lesions on the leaf surface as well as younger fruits. The spots are with irregular margins. During the favourable environment, many spots coalesce to form large patches of black colour on the infected fruit and leaf. The fungal hyphae do not penetrate deep into the fruit tissue. Sometimes the affected fruit get cracked and turn hard. The immature fruits fell off. There is longitudinal splitting of bark takes place. In

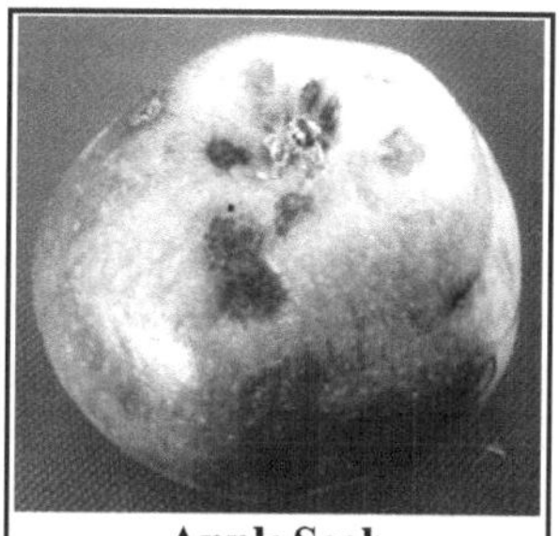
**Apple Scab**
**(*Venturia inaqualis*)**

severe cases the patches or the upper surface of the leaf shows brownish sooty mass of fungal hyphae (Tudzynski, 2005).

**Stem Gall**

The stem of infected coriander initially produces small protuberances which are gradually increased in size. In this way many galls are developed on the stem. The infection is systematic in nature. The premature galls are soft in touch and fleshy. Older fully mature galls become hard. Affected plant produce hypertrophied flowers and fruits (Schumann & D'Arcy, 2010). The disease is caused due to infection of *Protomyces macrosporus*, a pathogenic seed or soil borne fungus.

**Wire Stem**

The wire stems symptoms caused by *Rhizoctonia solani* to vegetable plant of cruciferae family. The characteristics features of wire stem symptoms are the seedlings get killed before emergence or after emergence. Initially dark brown coloured lesion develop on stem of infected plant which encircle the stem and becomes sunken, and later on it becomes rough and hard. The affected region becomes thin and delicate. This type of symptoms termed as wire stem. (Rimmer and van der Berg, 2007).

**Black Leg**

The infected plant shows oval, depressed, brownish, cankerous spots near the base of the stem. The spots increase until the stem is girdled. The affected tissue turn dark black, simultaneously circular brown spots develop on the leaves. The fully developed lesions show numerous dots also get infected and show similar symptoms. The black leg disease of cabbage is caused by *Phoma Lingam.*

**Black Scarf**

The stem canker phase responsible for drying and wilting of entire plant before they emerge. Externally the affected potato may show rough, black encrustations on which the fungus produces sclerotia, (Watt, 2010). The black scarf phase occurs later in which rough dry black encrustations are formed on affected tubers. The black scarf of potato is caused by *Rhizoctonia solani.* The distinct features of black scurf symptoms are the stem canker phase due to which the sprouts are killed before emerge and delays the germination, affecting the loss of yield. In the black scurf phase, the surface of potato tubers consists of rough, black encrustations. Such type of symptoms termed as black scurf. Exm: Black scurf disease of potato is caused due to Rhizoctonia solani.

**Black Scarf of Potato**

## Staghead

When the infected plant (shrub or tree) show drying of branches from top to bottom, the dried region consist of dead tissue. Such types of symptoms are termed as staghead. The staghead symptoms are caused due to fungal pathogens (Singh,1998).

## Shanking

The characteristic features of shanking are- the buds of infected plant shrivel and leaf tips turn to chlorotic. There is poor development of roots. In severe cases of diseases development, rotting of roots takes place. Rotting may extend into the base place. Shanking of tulip is caused due to infection of *Phytopthora cryptogea.*

## Wilt

The wilt diseases are mostly caused by soil borne fungi. In case of wilt disease, the infected plant becomes yellowish because of growth and accumulation of pathogenic fungus inside the xylem vessels of the infected host plant. The yellowing causes defoliation and at last the entire plant or plant part get dried.

**Wilt Disease of Pigeon Pea**

The infected plant show gradual loss of turgidity. The fungi causing wilt disease are facultative parasites. These parasites remains in soil on plant debris of previous crop in absence of host plant; and these infect and cause disease when the crop is sown in the field. The soil and seed or seed sets are the best sources of inoculum of the pathogens causing wilt diseases.

**The Wilt Disease of Gram**

The wilt parasite infects the root system of respective hosts. The pathogens are host organ specific. After infection to the root, the promycelium migrate towards the vascular tissue especially huge growth of fungal hyphae takes place inside the xylem vessels, transportation of water get affected. In severe cases of disease development vessels get blocked. Because of deficiency of water the infected plant turns yellowish and then heavy defoliation makes the plant like a broom. The affected plant dry up gradually which can be easily identified in the field. Exm: wilt disease of pigeon pea (*Cajanus cajan*) pathogen – *Fusarium udum*; wilt of cotton (*Gossypium arboretum*) pathogen- (*Fusarium oxysporum of sp. vasinfectum*); wilt of linseed (*Linum usitatissimum*) pathogen (*Fusarium oxysporum* f. sp. *lini*) (Pegg and Brady, 2002).

**Club Root**

Above ground level stunting of top of plant takes place. Plant remains short and do not head. Chlorosis and drooping of outer leaves may cause death of plant growth of abnormal growth of root system takes place. Affected parts of root may become more than 5 times larger than the normal are. The disease is caused by *Plasmodiophora brassicae* Woronin. It is a small piece of protoplasm which is called as plasmodium. It increases in quantity in presence of enough nutrition by the process of multiple fission. The alternate hosts of this pathogen are turnip, radish, mustard, rutabagas, cauliflower, sweet alyssum and shepherds purse etc.

## Pink Root

The distinguish features of pink rot symptoms are pink colouration of infected roots. Initially the rot get shriveled, die, and then a pink colouration is developed due to pigmentation in mature hyphal threads of fungus *Pyrenocheta terrestris*. Pink root symptoms observed in infected onion plant; the bulbs remain short, leaves of infected plant do not show normal growth.

## Hairy Roots

The root system of infected plant gets modified to a cluster of root hairs. The symptoms are termed as root hairs.

## Vascular Discolouration

The vascular tissue of plant affected by wilt disease causing fungus becomes reddish pink or browning due to interaction of pathogen with vascular elements. Such type of symptoms termed as vascular discolouration. Exm: *Fusarium* sp. causes wilt disease of *Cajanus cajan*.

In certain stress conditions, the central region of potato tubers turns to purple or red coloured due to pigmentation. Pigmentation is caused due to one or more than a physiological disorder. Externally the affected tuber turns green.

## Wart

The underground part of plant yet infected by pathogen. The infected cells multiply rapidly and produce hypertrophied mass of tissue resulting into abnormal growth on affected plant part. The hypertrophied portion may have beaded protuberances. Such symptoms are termed as wart. Wart may be soft, pulpy, spherical or wrinkled. The *Synchytrium endobiocticum* is a fungus causes wart disease of potato. (Sharma, 1971).

Black Scarf of Potato

## Fly Speak

The fly speck symptoms is characterized by development of definite, circular, black often glistening spots which resemble flyspeck. The moist weather is highly favorable for development of flyspeck symptoms. The Flyspeck disease of apple is caused by Gloeodes pomigena.

**Decline**

The decline symptoms are commonly observed in forest trees. The affected trees show progressive defoliation and drying of twigs. The infected treed die within 2-3 years of infection. The fibrous roots turn dark brown and finally die. The decline of cashew nut tree in caused by *Pythium spinosum.*

**Felt Disease**

The infected twigs and branches get encircled by soft felt like leathery growth of fungus which gradually extends to leaf bases, petioles and fruit stalks. The fungus does not penetrate the bark. The felk disease of citrus plant is caused due to infection of *Septobasidium pseudopedicellatum.*

**Grassy Stunt**

Infected plants remain stunted, that show profuse tillering thereby the plants resemble the grass. Such types of symptoms observed in rice due to infection of Nilapervata lugens.

**Witches Broom**

A broom like appearance of infected plant takes place due to infectious pathogenic organism. The infected plant shows branches with swollen base and the shoots usually all turned upwards, becomes short and possesses small leaves. Such type of symptoms termed as witches broom.

**Black Bundle**

The characteristic features of black bundle symptoms are the blackening of the vascular bundles visible as black dots on the cut ends of the stalk. In severe cases of disease development leaves dry up and plant may wilt. Ears get rotted. The black bundle symptoms caused by *Cephalosporium acremonium* in maize plants.

## Flattening of Branches

The branches of infected plant become flattened and twisted. The infected plants produce hard, small, shriveled fruits. Leaves turn yellow and thin leaves and fruits fell off before maturity. The flattened branches may give rise to normal branches. (Khurana & Singh, 1973). Flattening of branches of sapota is caused by *Botryodiploidia theobromae.*

## White Tip

The leaf tip of infected plant becomes chlorotic, die and turn white. The affected leaves hang down. Water soaked areas develop at the basal region of the leaf. The white tip symptoms of leak (*Allium porrum*) are caused by *Phytopthora porri.*

# 3

# Symptoms caused by Bacterial Pathogens

The bacteria are the single celled organisms. These are very small living entities rarely more than 0.01mm in length. They can be seen only with the higher powered of the microscope. Their cell walls are made with a complex mixture of protein, sugar and lipids. The cell is a typical prokaryotic type. The individual bacteria may be spherical, rod shaped or spiral and some have filaments called flagella. Some bacteria contain a photosynthetic pigment like chlorophyll but most of the bacteria live in or on their food. Bacteria release the enzymes outside the cell and absorb digested liquid food back in to the cell. The bacteria which need oxygen for their respiration are called aerobic bacteria, (Arnold, *et.al.*, 2003). Those which does not need oxygen for respiration is called anaerobic bacteria. The bacteria reproduce asexually by the method of fission. Sexual reproduction takes place by the method of conjugation of two cells of opposite strain. Bacteria cause diseases of plants, animals and human beings.

## The Ultra-structure of Typical Bacterial Cell

The bacteria are the very small organisms consisting of single cell rarely more than 0.01 µm. in lengths. The outer most layer of the bacterial cell is rigid, which is made up of protein, sugars and lipids and not of cellulose. The outermost layer is also enveloped by a layer of sticky substance that is known as the capsule. The capsule is made up of the combination of polysaccharides and polypeptides. The plasma membrane is situated inner side of the outer wall. The cytoplasm is placed to the inner side of the plasma membrane. The cytoplasm may contain granules of glycogen, lipid and other food reserves. The cell organelles like mitochondria, Golgi bodies and endoplasmic reticulum are absent. The cell consists of 70S type of ribosome's that are randomly scattered within the cytoplasm. Each bacterial cell contains a single chromosome which is highly coiled thread like in appearance that is freely suspended in the cytoplasm. The chromosome consisting of a circular strand of DNA. The chromosome is not enclosed in a nuclear membrane hence there is no nucleoplasm. All the above mentioned characteristics of the cell indicate that the bacterial cells are prokaryotic.

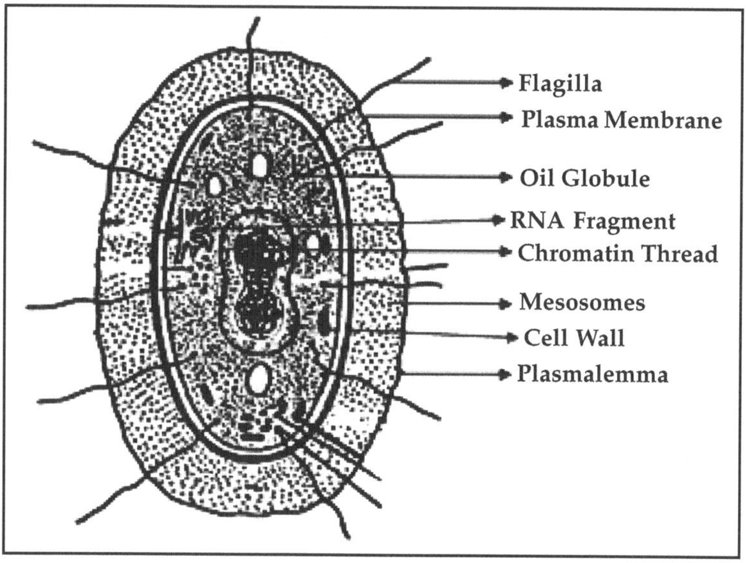


**An Ultra-structure of a Typical Bacterial Cell**

**Table 3.1: Plant Pathogenic Bacterial Genera and Symptoms**

| Sl. No. | Plant Pathogenic Bacterium | Symptoms |
|---|---|---|
| 1. | *Xanthomonas* | Leaf spots, leaf bight, canker |
| 2. | *Pseudomonas* | Leaf spot, galls, wilt, blight, canker |
| 3. | *Clavibacter* | Ear rot, stunting, canker |
| 4. | *Streptomyces* | Scab |
| 5. | *Curtobacterium* | Wilt |
| 6. | *Erwinia* | Soft rots, necrosis, wilts |
| 7. | *Rhodococcus* | Abnormal branching |
| 8. | *Corynebactarium* | Hypertrophy |
| 9. | *Agrobactarium* | Hypertrophy |
| 10. | *Ralstonia* | Vascular wilt |

## Symptomatology of Bacterial Plant Diseases

Most of the plants present on the world get affected by fungal pathogens. The pathogenic bacterium produces different types of symptoms on various ports of plant. The bacteria produces different type's signs on infected site on symptoms caused by bacteria are explained (Arnold, *et.al.*, 2003). The bacterial pathogens cause disease of number of plants. Which are host specific in nature. It also causes different types of symptoms infected plants. Some of the types of symptoms discussed below:

1. Lesions/spots
2. Angular leaf spot
3. Soft rots
4. Vascular wilt
5. Galls
6. Bacterial scabs
7. Bacterial wilt
8. Bacterial blight
9. Bacterial leaf blight
10. Canker
11. Bacterial Rot
12. Bacterial ooze
13. Stunting
14. Bacterial gall
15. Bacterial streak
16. Exudation
17. Chlorosis
18. Bacterial leaf scald
19. Citrus greening
20. Bleeding

21. Halo blight
22. Latexosis
23. Yellowing
24. Wild fire
25. Bacterial yellowing

**Bacterial Lesions or Spots**

A variety of crop plant show spots of various shape and size especially on leaf and fruits. The bacterial plant pathogens causing lesions are *Xanthomonas* and *Pseudomonas*. In severe cases the spots are formed on leaf petiole, stems, and on fruits of infected plant.

**Angular Leaf Spot**

The mature leaves are more susceptible. The infection to leaf show water soaked spot on the lower surface. The spots increase gradually which later turn to brown and form angular dead areas which are bounded by vein lets; and become visible on the upper surface. In severe cases the infection spread very fast. The leaf show elongated water soaked dark brown areas. Yellowing, rotting and drying of leaf tips are common (Verma and Singh, 1974). The leaves fell off and die. Angular dead areas occur which are visible on the upper surface of leaf.ead along the veins (Vein Blight) and reach to the petiole and then to the stem.

The pathogen produce elongated grayish to black lesions (Black arm), on the stem. The infected stem show several deep cracks from which a sticky substance comes out. The infected stem becomes delicate which break off easily. Affected branches dry. The spots formed on stem are linear and sunken, Angular leaf spot disease of cotton is caused by *Xanthomonas compesrtis.*

**Bacterial Soft Rot**

Soft rot symptoms consists of maceration of affected tissue, takes place. The soft rot occurs in the field or during storage mostly fleshy leaves, vegetables or soft rot symptoms due to bacterial infection. The cells wall of host tissue degraded by enzyme secreted by bacterial pathogens. The tissue emit foul odour. The infected fruits or leaves show toxic exudates which consists of bacterial pathogen. The bacteria pathogen causing soft rot disease includes certain species of *Erwinia* and *Pseudomonas.*

**Bacterial Vascular Wilt**

Numerous vegetables field crops and ornamental plant get affected with wilt pathogen. All the pathogenic bacteria are host specific in nature.

The bacteria which get nutrition from the vascular tissue of the host plant causes wilt disease. The important pathogenic bacteria causing vascular wilt of broad spectrum of plants are *Clavibacter, Cutobacterium, Erwinia, Pseudomonas* and *Xanthomonas.* The infected plant fell off and dries up. Some plants show stunting growth.

The underground plant parts get infected and sudden wilting and death of plant takes place.

Exm: Bacterial wilt of potato caused by *Pseudomonas solanacearum.*

**Tumours (Galls)**

The bacterial genera causing galls or tumours on to the host plants are *Agrobacterium, Pseudomonas, Rhizobactor, Rhodococus* etc. The infected tissue of host divide and many times farming a gall like structure. (Ryder and Jones, 1991).

**Bacterial Scabs**

The bacteria responsible for scan disease of the plant are Streptomyces; the scab disease of major importance caused by bacteria are scab of potato (*Streptomyces scabies*) Pox of sweet potato.

**Bacterial Wilt**

Several crop plants get affected by *Pseudomonas solanacearum* which show wilting at any stage of plant growth. Exm: *Pseudomonas solanacerum* causes wilt of vegetable crop of Solanaceae family. In wilting the affected plant turn reddish and brown and dry up or fell off. The wilt of banana is caused by *Fusarium oxysporum.*

### Bacterial Blight

Blight is the symptoms that are caused by bacteria or fungal pathogen resemble each other. Because the affected region consist of dead patches of host cells. Blight symptoms occur on stem, leaf or fruit except root system. Blight symptoms are mostly caused by *Xanthomonas* and *Pseudomonas* bacterial blight of rice.

Bacterial blight of plant is very common in temperate, subtropical and temperate region of the world. It is most severe and destructive in tropical regions, initially the infected plant part show many water soaked lesions which increase gradually and get mixed, and involve most of the part of leaf or stem, in advanced stages, the blighted regions consist of dead tissue, and the entire blighted region encircled with yellow chlorotic zone.

Exm: The genus *Xanthomonas* and *Erwinia* causes fire blight of apple (*Erwinia* amylovora).

### Bacterial Leaf Blight

The blight symptoms consist of large areas of dead tissue. Initially many spots are formed on infected leaf. In severe cases the spot increase in size and get mixed involving larger portion of leaf to blight. These are irregular in shape, size, and colour. The bacterial pathogens enter the leaf through stomata or injuries caused due to insect bite or mechanical agents.

### Canker

Canker is the lesions caused due to bacterial pathogen. Cankers are slightly raised, irregular, rough, necrotic, lesions occur on all parts of affected plant except root system. Canker symptoms surrounded by yellow hole of chlorotic zone. The cankers are mostly developed on barks or fruits. They are often large areas with definite margin. These are the spots consists of dead tissue. The affected region generally shows cracks and falls away Exm: *Xanthomonas citri* (Canker disease of citrus (lemon)).

### Bacterial Rot

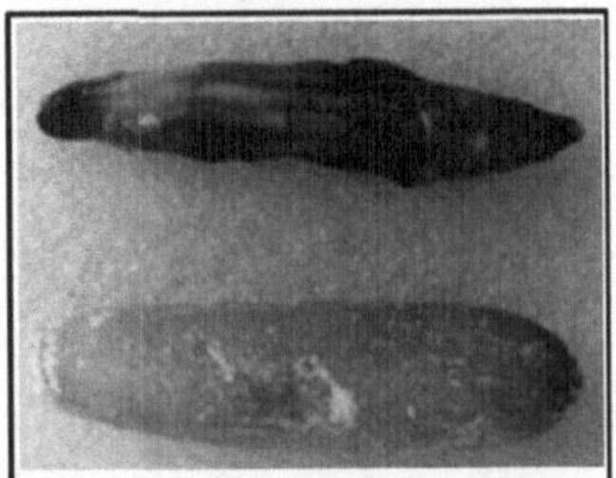

Bacterial Rot of Baby Carrots

The infected leaf of fruit initially shows a small water soaked spot which appear wet. Gradually the spot turns to sunken and increase in size by in evolving host tissue, and typical soft rot symptoms develop by bacterial pathogen. The infected plant part oozes watery substances which emit foul dour. Exm: Soft rot of potato (*Pseudomonas marginalis*).

### Bacterial Ooze

It is due to maceration of host tissue affected by bacterial pathogen. The infected fruits lose its turgidity because of degradation of cell wall. The soft skinned fruits are more susceptible. In severe cases of disease development the affected plant part specially fruits oozes watery substance which certain bacterial pathogen & macerated, host tissue.

### Stunting

Stunting are the symptoms in which the affected plant do not grow as non-infected plant grow. Plants remain short. Growth in retarded due to interaction of host and bacterial pathogen. Exm: Stunting of sugarcane caused by *Clavibacter sp.* the infected sugarcane secrete gummy semisolid substance from the nodal regions.

### Bacterial gall

The disease first appears as small outgrowth on stem, leaf, and root; initially galls are round, soft, white in colour. At maturity turn dark brown. Autonomous growth of tumor cells.

The bacterial pathogens causing gall disease of plants include *Agrobacterium, Pseudomonas, Rhizobactor* and *Rhodococcus* etc.

### Bacterial Streak

Especially it is a foliacious disease. At initial stage small water soaked areas develop on leaf. These enlarge gradually along the veins of infected leaf. After two weeks a characteristic yellowish coloured prominent bacterial bead get deposited in linear rows all along the veins. Sometimes several streaks may coalesce to form large blotchy lesions. Exm: Leaf streak of rice.

**Exudation**

These are the symptoms especially caused due to infection of bacterial pathogen. The infected fruits ooze out light coloured watery substance which is called as exudation. Exudation gets deposited on affected region which later turn to crust like structure. This watery substance emit foul odour.

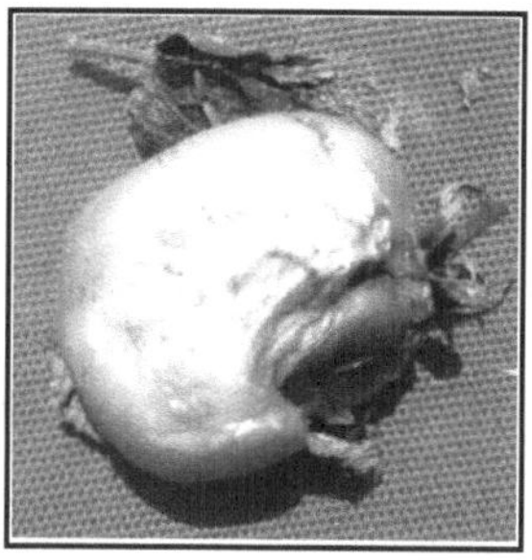

**Chlorosis**

The reduced functioning of chlorophyll results into a various kinds of chlorosis. The chlorosis may be due to mineral deficiency, viral disease, wilt, or any other agencies. Chlorosis may take place in the form of patches or streaks or entire leaf or whole plant sometimes shows chlorosis (Arthur, 1885).

**Bacterial Leaf Scald**

The bacterial leaf scald (scorch) of a variety of forest tree leaf is caused by *Xyllela fastiosa*. The leaf margins gradually turn reddish brown. The red brown scorch area consists of dead tissue (necrosis). The drying reach from margin to entire leaf & up to the petiole. Such symptoms affect the photosynthetic rate of plant. The yield in reduced to a great extent.

**Citrus Greening**

The infected plant possesses yellow coloured veins due to presence of bacterial pathogen inside the vascular tissue. The tissue which is present along the veins becomes yellowish due to development of pathogen inside the host. Gradually entire leaf turns yellow because of disturbances in functioning of chlorophyll. The *Candidus* sp. is a bacterial pathogen which causes citrus greening disease of citrus plant.

The infected plant remains short. Flowering takes place in off season. Most of the flowers of infected plant fell off. The twigs start drying from top to bottom. The root hairs and root let's get rotted. At last the entire plant gets dried. The infected fruits remains small, remain immature, and dark green in colour (Cao, *et.al.*, 2001).

### Bleeding

In certain infected fruits by bacterial pathogen, a thin transparent, clear or dark coloured or brownish watery substance is released out due to interaction of pathogen. Such type of symptoms affects greatly the morphological and biochemical status of infected fruit. Such types of symptoms are termed as bleeding or slime flux.

### Halo Blight

The infected leaf of French bean due to show water soaked which are distinct on lower surface of leaf. The spot increase in size and get mixed by farming large sized irregular patches. The spots are enriched with a characteristics yellow halo. The patches consist of dead tissue. Such type of symptoms caused by infection of bacterial pathogen, *Pseudomonas,* (Burrill and Jonathan, 1878).

### Latexosis

When the infected part of plant streams milky white fluid, such type of symptoms are termed as 'latexosis'.

### Wild Fire

The characteristic features of symptoms are the formation of prominent yellow holes with well defined margins around the central area of brown dead leaf tissue. In damp weather the spots increase in size and run together forming large brown dead areas on the leaf. Such types of symptoms are termed as wild fire. The wild fire symptoms are caused by *Pseudomonas tabaci* in soybean.

### Bacterial Yellowing

In case of infected leaf, when the chlorophyll disappears completely from the host tissue, the infected branch turn yellow and the symptoms are termed as 'yellowing'.

# 4

# Symptoms caused by Viral Pathogens

Most viruses are smaller than bacteria. Viruses can be seen with the electron microscope at the magnification about X 30000. Viruses can survive outside the host cell but in order to reproduce they must penetrate into a living cell. They vary in their shape and structure. Viruses have a central core of DNA or RNA surrounded by a protein coat. Viruses have no nucleus, cytoplasm, cell organelles or cell membrane. Virus particles therefore are not cells. Viruses do not feed, respire, excrete or grow. Viruses do reproduce but only inside the cells of living host organisms. Many viruses cause diseases of plants, animals and human beings.

The plant pathogenic viruses are ultra-microscopic simple structures composed of fragment of genetic material (nucleic acid) which is enveloped by protein coat. A numbers of economically important plants get infected by pathogenic viruses. There are about 2000 known viruses and about 977 are known plant viruses causing different types of diseases. Viruses causes a typical symptoms which are easily recognizable. Viruses causes, Leaf Curls, leaf roll, mosaic, yellow mosaic, vein mosaic, tungro symptoms, (Mansoor, *et.al.*, March 2003).

Table 4.1: List of Viral Diseases

| Sl. No. | Host | Pathogenic Virus |
|---|---|---|
| 1. | Elm (*Ulmus americana*) | Elm mosaic |
| 2. | Cowpea (*Vigna unguiculata*) | Cowpea mosaic |
| 3. | Black gram (*Vigna mungo*) | Black gram mettle |
| 4. | Bean (*Phaseolus vulgaris*) | Bean common mosaic |
| 5. | Peanut (*Arachis hypogoea*) | Peanut mettle |
| 6. | Soybean (*Glycine max*) | Soybean mosaic |
| 7. | Barley (*Hordeum vulgare*) | Barley Stripe |
| 8. | Alfalfa (*Medicago sativa*) | Alfalfa mosaic |
| 9. | Pea (*Pisum sativum*) | Pea enation mosaic |

## Symptoms Caused by Viruses

The viral pathogens cause different types of symptoms on host plants.

1. Chlorosis
2. Ring spot
3. Vein clearing
4. Vein banding
5. Necrosis
6. Curls
7. Mosaic
8. Viral crinkling
9. Viral Stripe
10. Bunchy top
11. Tungro
12. Leaf roll
13. Leek yellow stripe
14. Big vein
15. Epinasty
16. Star crack
17. Clump
18. Rosette
19. Tenosis or small leaf
20. Xyloporosis
21. Psorosis
22. Exocortis (Scally butt)

### Chlorosis

In case of mosaic diseases of plants, the chlorophyll disappears due to interaction of pathogen. Initially yellow spots are developed; such symptoms are called termed as chlorosis. The viral chlorosis is easily recognizable.

### Ring Spot

The affected plant possesses chlorotic rings on leaf, fruit or stem of respective host plant. Symptoms are termed as ring spots. Ring spot is a type of symptoms which is used to describe an irregular patchwork of green and yellow areas on the infected leaf surface. In certain cases the leaves may also become distorted. There is no distinct sharp margin occur between the affected and healthy areas of leaf. Ring spot is caused by viral pathogen.

Ring spot are caused by variety of fungal/bacterial pathogens. The symptoms are mostly formed on lower surface of leaf. A very small, round, with variable size and shape. In several cases many spots coalesce to form large necrotic patches. Exm: Ring spot of sugarcane (*Leptosphaeria sacchari*)

**Vein Clearing**

The interveinal region of leaf turn yellow, veins remain green. The symptoms termed as vein clearing or vein banding.

**Vein Banding**

A border of yellow tissue (chlorotic region) occurs along larger veins of the leaf of infected plant. Such types of symptoms are observed in viral diseases. Such types of symptoms are termed as vein banding.

**Necrosis**

Necrotic spots are also caused by viral pathogens. Spots of dead tissue develop on leaf surface which are randomly distributed. The other symptoms caused by viral pathogen in different types of plants are bunchy top, rolling, curling, crinkling, hypertrophy and atrophy etc.

**Curls**

The viruses are obligate parasites. There are numerous plant pathogenic viruses which are host specific in nature. The plant viruses infect all the parts of plant. The affected leaves show mosaic symptoms. In severe infected plant enroll downward; such symptoms are termed as curls. The viral pathogen *Phaseolus lycopersici* virus-I cause leaf curl disease of tomato. The leaf curl disease is very common in tropical regions of the world. Kallo *et.al*, (1986) reported 75% loss of tomato due to leaf curl disease. The symptoms include interveinal yellowing, vein clearing, crinkling and puckering of leaves. Curling of infected leaf reduces photosynthetic exposure of leaf to sunlight.

**Mosaic**

The leaf of infected plant show stunting, mottling and leaf malformation. Irregular shades of yellow or green are observed an infected leaves. Factors related with maturity of host, strain of pathogenic virus and environment might influence symptoms. Exm: Bean Mosaic.

The intervene area may turn chlorotic thus whole leaf becomes yellow. Mosaic disease is serious that is responsible for great losses of yield. The characteristic features of mosaic symptoms are formation of network of veins and vein lets:

***Enation Mosaic***

Enation mosaic of tomato is a viral disease. It is a type of mosaic in which the infected leaf shows pin head shaped rough outgrowth especially on the lower surface of leaf. The symptoms are caused by enation mosaic virus.

***Sterility Mosaic***

Sterility mosaic of pigeon pea is caused by pigeon pea sterility mosaic virus.

***Yellow Vein Mosaic***

The infected plants show mottling, yellowing of leaves and pods. The infected plants show reduced growth, remain stunted, which appear bushy. The infected leaves curl downwards, infection causes the drooping of flowers and the setting of the pods is delayed. The seeds may be aborted, remain smaller or malformed. The yield may be reduced up to 80 to 100 percent. The infected leaf possesses dark and light green areas and the leaf veins turn yellowish and clearly seen. The leaf

**Mosaic of Cucurbits**

areas showing the mosaic are generally irregular in outline. The affected areas may have two shades of colour i.e. dark green and yellow green (Mansoor, 2003). There are about 14 viruses of different groups that cause mosaic disease of different beans.

### Viral Crinkling

The affected fruits get shriveled which change their shape for some extent. Crinkling of apple is commonly observed.

### Viral Stripe

Viral stripe symptoms observed in rice infected by stripe virus. All the stages of plant growth are susceptible for infection. The leaves of infected plant possess yellow coloured stripes and streaks of dead tissue on the leaves. In case of severe infection, grey necrotic streaks develop on leaf. The affected leaf fell off in severe cases of disease development.

**Leaf Curl of Tomato**

### Bunchy Top

A typical viral symptoms observed in banana due to infection of banana bunchy top virus (BBTV) which especially grow in petiole, mid drib and veins. The infected leaf show dark brown streaks on petioles and veins and the leaf margin show chlorosis. The top-most leaves are narrow upright and are closely packed to give bunchy appearance. Exm: Bunchy top disease of banana (Banana bunchy top virus (BBTV).

### Tungro

The characteristic symptoms of tungro disease include stunting of infected plant. Discolouration of leaves, are very common. In some plants vein clearings formation of small, rusty, or necrotic spots are common. Exm: Tungro disease of Rice (Rice tungro bacilliform virus-RTBV). The infected plant remains short. Infected leaves turn yellowish. Interveinal chlorosis is common. It is a virus causing tungro disease in plants. Young leaves show light yellow chlorotic patches. Rough and brownish streaks develop on older leaves. In tungro disease root system show very poor growth. Exm: Tungro disease of rice (Virus).

**Leaf Roll**

The leaves of infected plant show downward rolling due to viral infection. In severe cases, most of the leaves get rotted, by the time, drop off, at any stage of its development. The affected plant becomes delicate, and yield in affected. The leaf roll disease of grapes is caused by leaf roll virus.

Tomato Leaf Curls

**Leek Yellow Stripe**

The infected plants remain short, turns yellow. The leaf lamina possesses irregular yellow striping; at the basal region. It is a viral disease. The plant becomes weak which is easily broken. The symptoms are termed as leek yellow stripe. The leek yellow stripe is caused by leek yellow stripe virus.

**Big Vein**

The characteristics features of big vein symptoms are clearing of vein. The affected plant becomes short or brushy. Such plant do not produce heads (cauliflower). It is a virus like agent.

**Epinasty**

The infected plants of part show curling or rolling or spiraled symptoms, the affected part of the plant bent downwards there is great variation in curling or rolling of plant parts in different plants. Such type of symptoms termed as epinasty. Downward curing of leaf or petiole are more distinct feature. There is variation in the epinasty according to the environmental factors.

**Star Crack**

The symptom mostly occurs on fruits surface. The infected fruit shows star-shaped cracks on the rind. Star cracks are also observed around the buds of infected plant. Exm: The star cracks of apple are caused due to viral pathogen.

### Clump

The infected plant show small dark green leaves and plants are severely stunted. The young leaflets shows mosaic mottling and chlorotic rings. Roots become dark coloured & outer layer peel off easily. Such types of symptoms are observed in groundnut due to viral infection (Ghanekar, 1980).

### Rosette

The affected plant remains short, which show bushy appearance as the nodes and internodes are shortened. There is reduction in leaflets. Plant produces small and sessile flowers which are useless. Rosette type of symptoms caused by viral pathogen in ground nut crop.

### Stenosis or Small Leaf

The characteristics features of stenosis symptoms are the infected plant show great reduction in size, leaves are greatly reduced and variously lobed. Flower becomes very small with non-functional ovary. Stenosis of cotton plant is caused due to infection of pathogenic virus.

### Xyloporosis

The infected plant becomes stunted with very small leaves. The pathogen causes the development of peg like outgrowth from the inner face of the bark that fit into corresponding pit like depressions in the stem. Gum pockets develop in the bark. Such types of symptoms are termed as xyloporosis. The xyloporosis of citrus is caused by viral pathogen.

### Psorosis

The characteristic symptoms on the infected trees are flecking in young leaves & scaling of bark on the branched & trunk region. The bark curls upwards and gumming takes place. The trees decline, leaves becomes smaller & yellow. The porosis symptoms are observed in citrus plants due to infection of pathogenic virus.

### Exocortis (Scaly Butt)

The infected plant gets stunted. The entire root system of trunk results in scaling of bark. The bark of the stem and twigs possesses large chlorotic blotches. The scaly butt symptoms are observed on citrus due to infection of viroids.

# 5

# Symptoms caused by Nematodes

The Nematodal parasites are widely present in soil, freshwater and marine water. Nematodes are the only plant parasites which belong to the animal kingdom. There are several hundred species of nematodes attack plants as a parasite and cause a variety of diseases (Cooke, *et.al.*, 2006)

The characteristics features of plant parasitic nematodes are: Excretory Canals (protoplasmic) presents, terminal excretory duct circularized, caudal glands absent, plasmids present, aphids usually minute, pore like and cephalic in position; sensory organs papillae, hypodermal glands absent, male with or without caudal glands.

The symptoms caused by soil borne nematodes are root galls, root knots, root lesions, excessive root branching, injured root tips etc. The nematodes which attack the aerial parts of the plant may cause discoloration, necrosis, blotches, spots, distortion and galls on leaf, stem, and seed (Bridge and Starr, 2007). The buds, growing points and flowering primordia are attacked by some nematodes causing abnormal growth of the affected region.

Table 5.1: The Nematodal Diseases of Plants

| Sl. No. | Diseases of Plants | Nematodal Pathogen |
|---|---|---|
| 1. | Root knot of vegetables | Many species of *Meloidogyne* |
| 2. | Molaya disease of barley and wheat | *Heterodera avenae* |
| 3. | Citrus root disease | *Tylenchulus semipenetrans* |
| 4. | Stem nematodes | *Radopholus* |
| 5. | Soybean cyst nematode | *Heterodera* sp. |
| 6. | Burrowing nematode | *Radopholus* |
| 7. | Bulb nematode | *Ditylenchus dipsaci* |
| 8. | Lesion nematode | *Pratylenchus penetrans* |
| 9. | Ear cockle nematode | *Anguina tritici* |

## Symptomatology of Nematode Pathogens

There are number of species of nematodes infect underground plant parts. The nematodes are present in soils which causes various diseases of plants. Thousands of species obtain food from plants as parasite. Wallace (1963) reported the list of plant pathogenic nematodes. It causes different types of symptoms after infection to host plants. Root galls, root knots, root lesions, excessive root branching, root rots, injured root tip, cyst ear cockle are the important symptoms.

Types of symptoms caused by plant pathogenic nematode:

1. Root knot
2. Ear cockle
3. Root lesions
4. Root rots
5. Excessive branching of roots
6. Galls & Tumor
7. Chlorosis
8. Tip burn
9. Tundu
10. Root pruning
11. Molaya

### Root Knot

The soil borne pathogenic nematode feed on root system of host plant. The nematode includes some secretion into the host cells which stimulate cell division; as a result small knots are developed. Indirectly it affects the growth of plant. Root knot nematodes are cosmopolitan in occurrence, which has a broad spectrum of host range. Root knot diseases of crop plants affecting the total yield of crop. These are the most prominent and easily recognizable symptoms. Root knot symptoms are characterized by formation of small outgrowths on root system of certain vegetables due to infection of soil borne nematodal pathogen. Exm: Root knot of vegetables caused is by meloidogyne.

### Ear Cockle

The ear cockle symptoms are caused by the nematode *Anguina tritici* on wheat. The seed in the main site of infection. Infected seed may have galls so the nematode is also known as seed gall nematode. The symptoms develop on all parts of the plant except root system. Affected plants remain stunted. Leaves show typical symptoms, which get rolled or twisted. The twisted leaf sometimes traps the new emerging leaf or inflorescence. Stems enlarge at the basal region. Infected heads become thick and short. Grains show galls which are filled by nematodal larvae. Most of the grains in the infected head get replaced by nematodal galls. These symptoms are termed as ear cockle.

The affected plants remain stunted and mostly show twisting of entire plant. The leaf blades split off twice or many times. The leaves of infected plant get twisted and stems show extra enlargement near the soil surface. The infected ear remains shorter and thicker. A dark black gall is formed at the place of grains due to infection. Only one or few of the grains are transformed into nematodal galls in the ear. The galls are hard structures consist of numerous larvae of the pathogenic nematode. The mature nematodal galls are shorter than the normal wheat grain (Townshend and Davidson, 1960). The ear cockle disease of wheat is caused by *Anguinia tritici* (stein) Filip Jev. It is a soil borne nematode. The pathogenic nematode is commonly called as seed gall nematode. Exm: Ear Cockle of wheat caused by *Anguinia tritici*

**Root Lesions**

The soil borne nematodes causes root lesion on affected plant root system. Initially a small water soaked spots are developed on root surface which later on turn to dark brown in colour. Such brown to black spots or lesions mostly develop on the younger roots. In severe cases many spots coalesce to form large sized lesions, and entire root system gets invaded. The lesions vary in size and shape. The lesions are probably caused due to toxic substance secreted by pathogenic nematode. Exm: *Padopholus, Pratylenchus etc.*

**Root Rots**

The soil borne pathogenic nematode feed on the root of plants. Due to feeding a wound is developed. Through the wounds the saprophytic fungi or bacteria enters the root causing rot symptoms of varying degree. Growth retardation, yellowing of leaf & dwarfness of affected plant takes place. Exm: root rot of banana caused by *radopholus similis.*

**Excessive Branching of Roots**

Certain pathogenic nematode inserts toxic substance into the root cells during feeding process. These substances induce formation of numerous short lateral branches by stimulating cell division. Many lateral branches arise from the root of nematodal injury.

**Galls & Tumor**

The gall is developed by fast multiplication of affected cell. The galls are formed on leaves, stem, fruit or inflorescence. The galls are globose or elongated or irregular large sized outgrowths which are formed on infected plant part. Exm: Club root of crucifers caused by *Plasmodiophora brassicae*; Crown gall diseases of plants caused by bacterial pathogen and root – knots caused by nematodal pathogen.

### Chlorosis

The reduced functioning of chlorophyll results into a various kinds of chlorosis. The chlorosis may be due to mineral deficiency, viral disease, wilt, or any other agencies. Chlorosis may takes place in the form of patches or streaks or entire leaf or whole plant sometimes shows chlorosis.

### Tip Burn

The soils borne plant pathogenic nematode enter the host plant by making hole onto the root system. Because of degradation of ground tissue of the root, the tips of root hairs get dried. The growing twig initially fades up and then turns yellowish. In severe cases of infection growing tips of twig get dried. Such types of symptoms are termed as tip burn.

### Tundu

The seedlings of wheat or rice are highly favorable for the pathogenic nematodal attack. The nematode cause's tundu disease is *Anguanea tritici.* The typical symptoms appear mainly on ear. The infected ear secret yellow coloured liquid. The leaves of infected plant show parallel yellow streaks along the veins. There is no grain formation in the ear. The leaves fade up. The infected plant becomes dwarf. Small chlorotic lesions develop on fruits. Such symptoms are termed as tundu or ear rot. Exm: Tundu disease of wheat and rice.

### Root Pruning

The root pruning is the symptoms in which there are no root tips to the affected plant. In certain nematodal diseases of plants the root tips of affected plant get feeded by nematodal pathogen. It is also termed as root tip necrosis.

### Molaya

Infected plant remains stunted. Plant have stiffer, thinner and narrower leaf blades than the healthy leaves. Tillering is greatly reduced. Culms become thinner and weaker. Early emergence of flower and formation of few grains in the ear takes place. Growing points of roots get killed. Such types of symptoms are termed as molaya.It is caused by pathogenic nematode *Heterodora avenae* in barly.

# 6

# Symptoms caused by Mycoplasma

Mycoplasma may be the simplest form of life capable of independent growth and metabolism. They are usually non-motile. Mycoplasma organisms are highly elastic and readily deformable that are without true cell wall hence Mycoplasma are irregular and variable in shape. The cells may be coccoid, granular, pear-shaped, cluster like, ring like or filamentous. The filaments may be branched or unbranched. There is so many variability in shape that no two forms are alike. The cells are small, ranging in diameter between 0.3 and 0.9µ. The Mycoplasma pass through many filters and grow on media which do not contain live tissues. the Mycoplasma are considered to be intermediate between bacteria and viruses. These organisms are covered with a unit lipoprotein cytoplasmic membrane, 7.5 – 10µ thick. The cytoplasm contains ribosome and nucleoplasm like structure. Though genetic material is composed of both DNA and RNA. Mycoplasma are Gram-negative and stain slowly on long exposure to dyes. These organisms reproduce by budding or binary fission. They are sensitive to Oxytetracycline, Streptomycin, Erythromycin and Chloramphenicol (Bertamini *et.al.*, 2004).

## Mycoplasma Diseases of Plants

The Mycoplasma is a free living parasitic organism, which resemble to a bacterial cell. It is a polymorphic spherical body of about 10 nm in diameter or large. It occurs in different forms. The parasitic forms of Mycoplasma cause diseases of plants.

The plant diseases caused by Mycoplasma are apple proliferation, papaya bunch top, aster yellow, blueberry stunt, brinjal little leaf, cherry buckskin, clover dwarf, citrus stubborn, corn stunt, grassy stunt of rice, legume little leaf, little cherry, little peach, lucerne witches broom, pea yellow dwarf, sandal spike, clover phyllody, sesamum phyllody, tobacco yellow dwarf etc.

All the diseases of plant of any family caused by Mycoplasma are grouped under the title "Mycoplasma diseases of plants".

**Table 6.1: Mycoplasma Diseases of Plants**

| Sl. No. | Host | Disease | Pathogen |
|---|---|---|---|
| 1. | Carrot<br>Onion<br>Tomato | Aster yellow<br>Aster yellow<br>Aster yellow | Phytoplasma |
| 2. | Coconut | Lethal yellowing | Phytoplasma |
| 3. | Perch | Peach X-disease | Phytoplasma |
| 4. | Pear | Pear decline | Phytoplasma |

## Types of Symptoms Caused by Mycoplasma

Mycoplasma is unicellular prokaryotic amoeboid organism causes different types of plant diseases. The symptoms caused by Mycoplasma' pathogen are listed below:

1. Little leaf
2. Yellows
3. Grassy shoot
4. Big bud
5. Phyllody
6. Grassy shoot
7. Fasciculation
8. Spike
9. Suppression
10. Rosetting
11. Top roll
12. Witches broom
13. Aster yellow
14. Decline symptoms
15. Grassy shoot
16. Rubbery wood
17. The burn

### Little Leaf

The pathogen affects the growth of plant. The leaves of affected plant get reduced in size and shape. Exm: Little leaf disease of brinjal caused by Mycoplasma. Affected plant does not produce fruits or it produces very small sized fruits.

### Yellows

The infected plant show disturbance of the chlorophyll. The leaf turns yellow due to loss of chlorophyll. The symptoms are termed as yellowing.

### Grassy Shoot

The infected plants appear like a bunch of grass. The affected shoot becomes short and yellow. Exm: grassy shoot of sugarcane.

### Big Bud

In case of infected plants the fruit producing shoot becomes thick and straight, it appears like a big bud.

### Phyllody

The inflorescence of infected plant malformed into leafy structures. Such flowers are sterile. The stamens also become leaf like. Ovary gets modified into long shoot like structure. Infected plant remains short in height and many abnormal branches produced by plant so it appears like a bush. The infected plant possesses green leaf like modification of floral parts. The phyllody types of symptoms are mostly caused by Mycoplasma (Lee, *et.al.*, 2000).

The phyllody types of symptoms are mostly caused by Mycoplasma. The inflorescence gets converted into leafy structures. Flowers become sterile. The stamens turn leaf like. Ovary gets modified into long shoot like structure.

### Grassy Shoot

The infected plant shows grassy appearance. Leaves turn yellowish white, entire shoot resemble like a small leafy bush. Such symptoms are induced in affected plants due to infection of *Phytoplasma*, which is a prokaryotic amoeboid pathogenic organism. Exm: Grassy shoot disease of sugarcane (*Phytoplasma*).

### Fasciculation

The infected part of plant show excessive branching due to attack of pathogenic Mycoplasma. Such types of symptoms are termed as fasciculation.

### Spike

The spike is the type of symptom in which the infected plant may have greatly reduced size of leave and greatly reduced nodes and internodes. The entire infected plant appears leafless. A severely infected plant dies within few months due to infection of phytoplasma which is insect transmissible pathogenic organism.exm: a spike disease of sandalwood is caused by phytoplasma.

### Suppression

The infected plant becomes abnormal in form and size. The plant does not show normal development of parts of plant. No any part is formed. The symptoms are termed as suppression.

### Rosetting

The stem of infected plant fails to increase in length, the cluster of leaves arise from such a highly reduced stem close to soil surface. Such type of symptoms termed as Rosetting. Rosetting symptoms are caused due to biotic pathogens.

### Top Roll

A variety of plants shows top roll symptoms which is caused by pathogenic organism Phytoplasma. The infected twigs and leaves get rolled from the top to bottom. The infected region turns to purple or pink in colour due to interaction of host and pathogen. The infected plant becomes dwarf. There should be profuse growth of axillary branches. The purple top rolls disease transfer through grafting. The infected tubers develop hairy outgrowth. Exm: top roll of potato is caused by Phytoplasma.

### Witches Broom

There are many factors responsible for witches broom disease of plants. The infected plant produce cluster of short weak branches which arise from a single point. In severe cases of disease development, the infected plant dry up gradually from top to bottom. The witches broom disease mostly occurs in deciduous s and evergreen trees as well as shrubs.

### Aster Yellow

It is a serious disease of most of the vegetables caused due to phytoplasma. The pathogen causes vein clearing and involves entire leaf. All the stages of leaf growth are highly susceptible for disease. These younger leaves turn chlorotic dry up gradually. Exm: Aster yellow of vegetables (*Phytoplasma*).

### Decline

Decline of affected plant takes place due to infection of Phytoplasma in this case a slow and steady drying of affected plant takes place. Exm: Pear decline. (*Phytoplasma*).

### Grassy Shoot

The infected shoots turn grassy and profusely tillering. Different types of symptoms are seen at different growth stage of the host plant. The disease is also known as albino disease, chlorotic disease or leaf stuff disease. The infected shoots remain stunted and dwarfed. Their canes remain thin with relatively short internodes and the leaves turn small and narrow. Thus the shoots developing from infected seed set gives a bunchy or grassy appearance. Hence the disease is named as "grassy shoots". The infected leaves loose chloroplast and become almost white. Sometimes leaves turn yellowish due to partial loss of chlorophyll. Later on the shoots having such white or yellow leaves dry up. The lowermost node produces large number of grassy shoots. The infected leaves show linear, light green or white or yellowish streaks. The infection induces change in anatomy and biochemistry of infected tissue. There are reports of inhibition of enzyme of sucrose synthesis. The disease is caused by a *Phytoplasma* (Singh, 1954)

## Rubbery Wood

Apple shoots infected by Mycoplasma possesses rubberness of shoots. The infected branches become flaccid and bend down. Twigs become flexible. Formation of leaves & blossom delayed. Leaves turn yellowish.Exm: Rubbery wood symptoms occur in apple tree due to infection of pathogenic Mycoplasma.

## Tip Burn

In case of infection by pathogenic Mycoplasma to host plant, in certain cases the tip of infected leaf dry up gradually from top to bottom. The leaves get distorted in shape necrosis appears along the margins of the blade. The leaf blades may cup downward or upward. Such type of symptoms termed as tip burn.

# 7

# Symptoms caused by Abiotic Factors

A major loss of crop also takes place by non-pathogenic diseases. Non-infectious diseases of plants are caused by the absence of any important life supporting factor or presence of that factor in excess. The non-infection or non-parasitic diseases cannot be transmitted from one diseased plant to healthy plant. For a long duration it was believed that the diseases are caused by adverse environmental factors, but recently it has became clear that the non-parasitic diseases in plants are due to environmental pollution and debris from nuclear weapons. The list of non-parasitic disorders of plants is as follows:

1. Injury
2. Cracks
3. Sunscald
4. Sudden death
5. Leaf tatter Leaf scorch
6. Odema
7. Pallor
8. Drooping

The non-parasitic diseases are also caused by mineral deficiency. The symptoms caused by non-parasitic diseases are discussed as follow:

**Injury**

Injury to the plants occurs in different ways. During pre-harvest treatment of crop injuries caused during the process of weeding. In India weeds are removed by a specific assessor called (*khurpe*) sometimes that injure the main plant part. Such injured plants have to face other problems like attack of soil borne fungi and other saprophytic organisms. Because of medicinal injury health of plant declines. During harvest of tuberous vegetables or tuberous rhizomes of medicinal importance, there are great possibilities of mechanical injuries to the crop. The injured produce loose market value hence great responsible for great economic losses. The vegetables plants having spines also get injured by their own spines during rough handling at the time of harvest. Especially this occurs in case of eggplant, when they collected in a container during harvest time. The injuries cause death of the plant because the injury becomes a way to enter pathogenic microorganism.

In the region of Kashmir and another snow fall regions of India, plant injuries observed due to snow fall and its accumulation, especially in case of evergreen plants, the breakage of leaves, buds and twigs takes place due to long term deposition of ice on the plant part. Sometimes because of increasing weigh of snow fall the branches of healthy trees and shrubs broken-down. The herbaceous ground flora and lichens also get disturbed due to heavy snowfall. Sometimes scales of Lichen break and fall on the ground due to continuous heavy ice fall. The ground herbs got enveloped by ice. Cold temperature injuries to plant also caused during transplantation of plants from one place to another, if the environment consists of severely cold temperatures, because the roots get exposed severely cold environment hence freezing and drying injuries occur in the transplants, such injuries also responsible for destruction of plants.

The injuries to the ornamental trees and shrubs in the gardens are caused due to careless handling of garden mowers and edge trimmer's machines like. Which are used for grass cutting and leveling for the purpose of cleanliness and beauty of gardens.

### Cracks

In this case the bark of trees /shrubs split open. This occurs mostly during rapid decrease in climatic temperature. The cracks are also formed due to previous injury to the stem of plant. The crack formation in trees barks in tropical and subtropical region in observed due to increase in temperature, disappearance of moisture from air. During severe winter season the cracks may become wider. Many of the tree plants secrete gum through the split open space. Many of them get injured through the cracks. Such cracks sometimes get closed due to formation of callus. Mostly the callus is formed in summer days. The cracks are deep mostly narrower, sometimes becomes wider and are deep up to the bark only.

### Sunscald

The bright sun-rays penetrate the bark of the tree for whole day and in the evening after sunset the temperature fall rapidly; that adversely affect the tissue of the bark. Young growing trees and soft thin barked trees and shrubs found more susceptible to sunscald injury. Mostly the tissues at the affected area get killed.

### Sudden Death

Red Pine is a timber yielding important tree of the Northern and Central states of America. The Connell University Ithaca reported a sudden death of red pine mature, stately trees in apparently excellent health suddenly dies. Trees begin to become weak for several years before they die. Several factors responsible for the cause. It has noted that, the decline and death of red pine appears to be associated with "Wet feet" problem, that is in which the affected root systems are growing in soil are in variably shallow and poorly drained. In such soils most of the roots are confirmed to the upper 6 inches of soil. Typically these root systems are in various stages of deterioration. The shallow and poorly declined topsoil. Appears to be responsible for triggering the decline of red pine.

During the years of high rainfall soil on these sites becomes so saturated that roots are starved of oxygen and suffocate. In the summer, the recovery of the root system is possible. During the periods of prolonged periods of high spring soil moisture continue several years, so that the diminished root system eventually losses its ability to nourish the growing crown and decline begins.

Old red pines are more susceptible because of their large size of crowns and root system. Too much or too little water around the tree system appears to lead to dieback of roots, and less development of branches.

**Leaf Tatter**

In very cold areas of the world plant face to frost injuries. The freezing injury to the leaves causes numerous holes to the leaf or a tattered appearance. The leaves showing this injury remain on the tree for long period. The plant with numerous such leaves looks unhealthy and delicate. Tender young leaves are more susceptible to freezing injury. Sometimes the injury in severe cases kills the leaves. In general, the freezing injury is not detectable until the leaves are fully expanded. The frost killed areas appear as prominent holes. The frost injured leaves do not show perfect growth in comparison to other non-injured leaves. Sometimes uneven growth also frequently contributes to a distortable appearance of the injured leaves. The badly tattered leaves will fell off early, and new leaves are formed on such young shoots of plant, hence this injury does not usually seriously harm the tree.

**Leaf Scorch**

Leaf scorch is a physiological problem that can occur in any kind of plant. The factors causing leaf scorch are due to soil compaction, nutrition deficiency, and more exposure of plant to the environment during transplantation, chemical injury, poor soil or limited space for root development and proliferation. Leaf scorch also occurs when the root system cannot get enough water. Hot dry environment increases the severity of leaf scorch especially just before summer days.

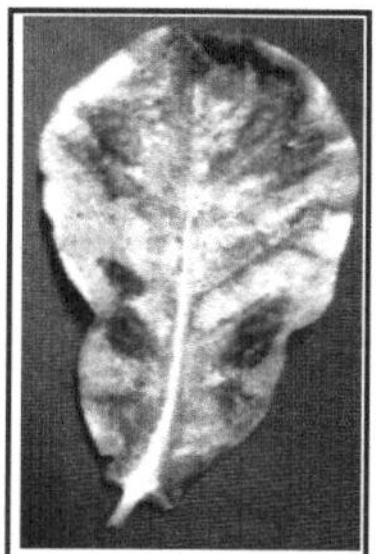
Leaf Scorch

The affected leaf tissue becomes yellowish due to upper functioning of chlorophyll. The yellowing extends gradually towards the healthy region of leaf. Later on the yellowing replaced by necrotic zone (dead tissue) hence the region of leaf tissue is brown in colour. The leaf scorch symptoms start from margin of the leaf or anywhere on the leaf. Sometime dark angular spots are formed in the discolored areas. The affected leaves fell off. The affected plant also shows same twig dieback.

### Odema

Odema is a type of symptoms in which small spots or corky blisters are formed on any part of plant excluding roots. Odema of root occurs when roots take up water faster than it can be used by the plant. The water pressure builds up in the mesophyll of the leaf resulting into a small raised blister on leaf. The blister occurs mostly on lower surface of leaf. These spots gradually become hard to form whitish or brown coloured warty growth on affected region. In severe cases the corky growth also occurs on petals, petioles and stem. According to the report of "The plant Disease Diagnosis Centre" Ithaca New York, the Odema is most prevalent in the late winter especially during extended period of cool, cloudy weather. It likely to develop when the soil is warm and moist and the air is cool and moist. Such an environment is responsible for rapid water absorption from the soil and slow water loss from the leaves. The certain fleshy leaved plant, are sensitive to such non –parasitic disease. Vegetables like cabbage and tomato can also be affected.

### Pallor

Pallor is a type of symptoms which is caused due to various non-parasitic agencies or biotic like algae. It is the yellowing of leaf which possesses the pathogen internally or externally on the yellow spot. If the pallor is developed due to non-parasitic pathogen, it shows only yellow spots, without any pathogenic organism.

### Drooping

Drooping symptoms are observed in a variety of plants due to biotic or abiotic causes. The leaves infected by *Cercospora, Alternaria* etc. droop off in severe cases of disease development. Drooping of fruits is caused by the attack of *Phytopthora* on palms.

### Symptomatology of Air Pollutants

Harmful gases cause various symptoms of plants. The gases harmful to plants are Hydrogen fluoride, ozone, ethylene, sulphur dioxide, chlorine, nitrogen dioxide, and dust smog, fly ash, brick kiln fumes and peroxy acetyl nitrate etc.

1. **Sulphur dioxide:** Margin of leaf turns necrotic

   Exm: Trees which occur around road side. Leaf chlorosis and bleaching of internal tissue of leaf.
2. **Ethylene:** It causes defoliation, irregular flower opening and affect plant growth.
3. **Flourine:** Causes necrosis of leaf margins.
4. **Ozone:** It causes weathering of plant. Interveinal necrosis of plants. Exm: Weathering of leaf surface of tobacco.
5. **Petroyacetyl nitrate:** Affected leaf turn silver glazing of the lower leaf surface. Exm: Spinach shows such symptoms.
6. **Chlorine:** It causes interveinal and marginal ($Cl_2$). Injury to affected leaf. Affected area turn to dark brown due to death of cells.
7. **Nitrogen oxide:** Affects the growth of plant. ($N_2O$)
8. **Hydrogen flouride:** The affected plants leaf show light green coloured water soaked lesions at initial stage. At maturity the spots turn reddish brown in colour.
9. **Dust:** Dust from the air deposit on leaf surface causing crusty appearance of leaf, later develop chlorotic patches, leaf show poor growth and necrotic spots.

### Oxides of Nitrogen

Some plants are sensitive to nitrogen dioxide. It causes chlorosis of leaves in severe cases grayish water soaked spots develop on leaf surface.

1. **Fluorides:** Exposed plant to fluoride gases possesses tan coloured scorching of leaf margins. Narrow chlorotic bands develop between living and dead region of plant part.
2. **Sulphur dioxide:** It is one of the most important phototoxic pollutants, the plant exposed to sulphur dioxide causes foliar necrosis.
3. **Ammonia:** Ammonia injury to plants causes irregular necrotic regions on leaf.

### Symptoms of Plant Disorder due to Air Pollution

The spots caused by air pollutant are relatively uniform in colour and interface between the affected parts of plant. Only those parts of plants get affected which is directly in contact with air pollution. There are two types of air pollution:

1. Hollow Heart
2. Bronzing

#### *Hollow Heart*

The symptoms are characterized by the development of hollow space in the centre of affected tubers. The size of cavity or hallow spaced may be variable in size and shape. Such symptoms are termed as hollow heart or hollow centre.

The cavity is developed due to death of pith cells, in the central region o tuber. As the tuber grow in soil, simultaneously the hollow heart is caused due to adverse effect of oxygen relations, during growth of tubers.

#### *Bronzing*

The infected plant show patches of dead tissue. The patches are bronze coloured. Hence the symptoms are termed as bronzing. Bronzing occurs due to adverse effect of environmental pollution or due to adverse effect of pesticides.

## Symptoms of Disorders due to High Temperature

The plant grows in open land. Plants can tolerate a great fluctuation in temperature. But very high or low temperature induces typical disorders in the morphology and physiology of suffering plant. Some examples of disorders caused due to high or low temperature given below. At low temperature potato tubers become sweetened. At very high temperature black scarf disease develops in stored potatoes, due to insufficient oxygen. The freezing injuries are commonly observed in banana, citrus, cucurbits, eggplants, sweet potato, pepper and potatoes' dark brown coloured rotted patches are developed on the affected fruit or fruit vegetables. A very high temperature causes sunscald of fruits and leaves, cankers on stem. At very high temperature seeds fail to germinate in soil. The post-harvest products especially fruits and vegetables appear to be more susceptible to high temperature stress; high temperature causes sun scald of apple in which the brownish patch in developed on the skin. Below the spot the pulp turn brown in colour. Such fruits are unfit for consumption. High temperature causes blossom end rot diseases of water melon.

## Symptoms Caused by Low or High Temperature

1. Sun scald
2. Sun burn
3. Yellow top
4. Blossom drop
5. Green back
6. Ring necrosis
7. Net necrosis
8. Blindness
9. Leafiness
10. Bolting
11. Mummy
12. Doubling of bulbs

### Sun Scald

Sun scald is a type of symptoms develops on fruits and fruit vegetables due to adverse effect of high temperature. Initially a water soaked spot develop on the affected fruit which gradually turn to a sunken spot due to rapid desiccation. It possesses white rough tissue. Sunscald symptoms also develop on leaves. All the stages of leaf and fruit growth are susceptible for sunscald symptoms. The affected leaf show chlorotic blotches on leaf lamina. The leaves and fruits possessing sunscald symptoms become susceptible for host specific bacterial and fungal pathogens. Such fruits become unfit for consumption.

### Sun Burn

When the fruits get exposed to sunlight for a longer duration, such fruits show patches of white dead tissue. Fruits become wrinkled. Wrinkling may be on entire fruits. Such fruits become highly susceptible for secondary infection of bacterial and fungal pathogens.

### Yellow Top

It is a type of symptom observed especially on the tomato fruits which are exposed to cool or hot temperature for longer duration. In this case a yellow patch is developed on the shoulder of affected tomato fruits.

### Blossom Drop

The blossom drop symptoms are observed in a variety of fruit crops because of exposure to high temperature and scarcity of water. There is no setting of fruits and the exposed blossom drop off. Such types of symptoms are termed as blossom drop.

### Green Back

The affected tomato possess dark green colour of stem and region and remaining fruit is yellowish red. This caused due to high temperatures. Due to high temperature gradual ripening is restricted and mother end of fruit becomes green. These types of symptoms are termed as green back.

### Ring Necrosis

It is also a disorder of potato tubers exposed to freezing temperature. In this case the vascular bundle gets affected; hence a necrotic symptom appears like a ring. Such the affected vascular bundles consist or brown coloured dead cells. Such type of symptoms termed as ring necrosis.

### Net Necrosis

The net necrosis symptoms develop in potato tubers when exposed to freezing temperatures. In this case the element of vascular tissue gets affected. Such a disorder in termed as net necrosis. There intensity of net necrosis is more pronounced at the region of attachment of potato.

**Blindness**

The symptoms blindness is characterized by cauliflower plants without the terminal buds. Instead of terminal buds large dark green, thick and leathery foliage in developed. According to Lee and Cardous (1949), this is a physiological disorder which is caused due to low temperature at very initial stage of plant development.

**Leafiness**

It is believed that the production of very small malformed leaves in the affected cauliflower which is due to prevalence of high temperatures. The symptoms are termed as leafiness.

**Bolting**

Exposure of growing seedling of cauliflower to low temperatures for longer duration, affected the normal flowering of plant. A premature flowering can be developed. Such types of symptoms are termed as bolting.

**Mummy**

The mummy symptoms are common in a variety of soft skinned fruits. The infected fruit show discolouration and shriveling. The mummy symptoms are caused due to adverse effect of temperature or fungal infection. There is great biochemical changes occur in affected fruit. Quality reduction reduces the cost of fruit. Gradual Shriveling and drying of fruit are the characteristic symptoms of mummy.

**Doubling of Bulbs**

Doubling of bulbs of onion observed in the field with poor soil fertility. Mechanical injury during cultural practices may also cause doubling in bulbs, (Choudhary, 1967).Other factors responsible for doubling of onion bulbs are water scarcity at initial growth stage and irrigating after a long duration of drought period.

**Symptoms of Adverse Effect of Environment on Plant Health**

The occurrence development of plant diseases are greatly influenced by weather. The diseases will not occur even in presence of proper host plant and respective pathogenic fungus together if the environmental conditions are not favorable. Environmental factors play a very important role in growth and development of pathogen on or inside the host plant. In certain cases the diseases the adverse environmental factors create problems in growth, development and reproduction of plants, which are called as non-parasitic diseases. The adverse environment induces a variety of symptoms in plants or plant parts.

**Symptoms of Adverse Effect of Environment**

1. False rust
2. Pox
3. Tip burn
4. Hollow leaf stalk
5. Cracks
6. Grey wall
7. Green shoulder
8. Hollow root

**False Rust**

During cold moist environmental conditions and due to metabolic alteration in affected Asparagus plant, long reddish streaks are developed along the stem. These streaks resemble the rust symptoms but it is not a caused due to rust disease causing fungi. Hence, the symptoms are termed as false rust.

**Pox**

The affected fruit possesses many small greenish specks of about 2-3 mm in diameter, which are scattered all over the fruit surface. In severe cases of pox development, many specks coalesce to for a large dark brown coloured sunken spot. Such type of disorder in termed as pox. This is developed due to environmental pollutants.

**Tip Burn**

In certain vegetable crop plants, the affected plant show dried leaf tips, dried leaf margins due to adverse environmental factors such as excessive drought or insufficient water during growth of plant. The affected area consists of dried tissue. Indirectly the tip burn symptoms affect the photosynthesis of plant. The tip burn region extends slowly from tip to base of leaf. The fully affected leaf or leaflets dry up and fell off. There is variation in the amount of tip burn. The older leaves are more susceptible for tip burn disease. All the above mentioned abnormality in plant is termed as tip burn.

### Hollow Leaf Stalk

The petioles of Celery vegetable leaves become hollow due to over maturity. The symptoms are termed as hollow leaf stalk.

### Cracks

Milad and Shackel (1992) reported the reason of fruit cracking is due to physical failure of fruit skin. The cracking symptoms are common in most of the soft skinned fruits. The characteristic features of crack symptoms are rupturing or split opening of fruits. The crack initiates from mother end region and extend to other end region of fruit. The crack may be up to certain centimetres or in mm. It causes loss of quality of fruit. Frazier (1947) reported that cracking of tomato was severe due to excess of irrigation at the end of prolonged dry weather. Several types of cracking occur in fruits:

(a) **Radial cracking:** Cracking initiate from peduncle region which appear star shaped.

(b) **Concentric cracking:** A crack develops from peduncle region in circular region.

(c) **Cuticle cracking:** Cuticle cracking (Russetting)

Radial cracking is common in young fruits of tomato. Concentric cracking is common in fully mature tomato fruits. The rainy season is more favourable for cracking tomato fruits.

### Grey Wall

The affected fruit show grayish-brown discolouration on the fruit surface. Small immature tomatoes. The affected area becomes rough and slightly depressed. Below the spot the fruit show internal browning, due to destruction of tissue. It causes great biochemical alteration, due to which affected fruits becomes unfit for consumption.

### Green Shoulder

The affected fruit show green yellowish colour on shoulder region, which is coarse in texture. Such type of symptoms observed tomato's. The symptoms are termed as green shoulder.

### Hollow Root

It is caused due to imbalance in soil moisture. The roots of affected plant remain hollow (Kranhnstover *et.al.*,1997).

### Symptoms Caused by Adverse Effect of Light on Plant

The intensity of light also controls the vegetation of particular area to a large extent. The land plants grow over an enormous range of light intensities. If a proper duration of light is not received, there will be fluctuation in occurrence of vegetation. The adverse effect of light is observed in case of many of the pre-harvest crop plants and as well as in Post-harvest vegetables and fruits.

Light is very important factor which is correlated with development of plant. The concentration of elements are influenced by light intensity, its duration and temperature extremes. Light affects the photosynthesis of plant and after the ratio of elements to dry matter due to dilution effects. Light through photosynthesis provides energy for active uptake of elements thus enhancing the concentration. The increasing light exposure reduces the N, P, and K concentration, but Ca concentration may increase. Hence light play important role in plant life. Adverse effect of light causes different types of diseases and symptoms in the affected plant.

### Symptoms Caused by Light

1. Etiolation; and
2. Greening of Tubers

### Etiolation

The plants growing in poor light intensity possesses pale yellow coloured leaves. The growth is restricted. Stems break off easily. Such plants remain stunted due to lack of enough light. The symptoms are termed as Etiolation. Light intensity is one of the important factors in the growth of plant. Variation in the amount of light can affect the host physiology. Insufficient light intensity affects the formulation of chlorophyll in the leaf. Plant growing in poor light intensity may have delicate stem & reduced leaf size. Low intensity of light during a plant growth causes drooping of flowers & premature leaves. This type of condition is called as etiolating. Because of deficiency of enough light the affect plant show or plant part show abnormal elongation, spindly, yellowish. Such symptoms are termed as Etiolation.

### Greening of Tubers

The affected potato tubers turn green in colour due to prolonged exposure to light or sunlight during storage or transportation. There is production of chlorophyll in the epidermal layer of potato tubers due to sunlight. Such type of symptoms termed as greening, which reduces market value (Lewis and Rowberry1973).

### Symptoms Caused by Freezing Injury

Meryman (1966) reported number of disorder of post-harvest perishables due to freezing injury. Fleshy leafy vegetables and fruits are highly susceptible than dry seeds to freezing injury. Freezing depression is due to the solute occurrence within the cell. The seed and nuts are no fleshy which can tolerate freezing temperatures, so there is no more damage. The water content of fleshly fruits & vegetables get deteriorated due to conversion of water into ice. Ice is formed in the cells & between the cells of infected host.

### List of Symptoms Caused by Freezing Injury

1. Fruit rot
2. Cracks
3. Cat face

## Fruit Rot

Fleshy fruits are highly susceptible to the freezing injury. Mostly fruits are stored in cool. There is variation in tolerance capacity of fruits to coolness. Excess of cooling causes freezing depressions (spot) due to the solute occurrence within the cell. Initially a light brown spot is developed on the fruit which increase in size. It caused fermentation of fruit juice. Such type of rot symptoms are observed in fruits stored for longer duration to higher level of cooling than the point of tolerance point of fruit.

## Cracks

The infected part of plant split open due to any adverse environmental factors or due to physiological disorder. The symptoms are termed as cracks. Mostly crack symptoms are commonly obtained in case of fruits and fruit vegetables stored in refrigerator.

## Cat Face

It is a type of symptom mostly occurs on fruits as well as vegetable fruits due to several reasons like very cool environment during flowering and fruit setting or due to excessive heat, pruning, erratic moisture or any other adverse environmental factor. The infected fruit may get fade up, may have ridges, furrows and blotches at certain regions. The tissue at mother end point turn brown to black in colour due to death of cells, it appears slightly raised and corky which gradually extend in all direction covering 70 to 80% region of fruit which resemble a cat face. Hence the symptom is termed as cat face.

## Symptoms of Moisture-inducer Disorders

Plants show symptoms due to lack of moisture or excess of water, for longer duration. If there is stagnant water present in the field it is responsible to cause causes tip burn of paddy because stagnant water reduces oxygen supply to root system. Excess of water induce wilting due to lack of oxygen supply to root system of host plants.

Loss of 5-10% water from post-harvest vegetables and fruits cause loss of turgidity and firmness. In addition to these other undesirable quality changes occur. Water loss causes discolorations of leafy vegetables, loss of colour, aroma, flavour and nutritional value. Excess water results when the harvested grains stored at high humidity, many saprophytic organisms grow on food grains and loss of entire lot of grains occur due to toxic substance secreted by saprophytic microorganisms. Various morphological and physiological changes occur in the commodity.

**Shedding of Flowers**

The flowers of plants fell off at any stage of its development due to very high or low temperature accompanied by low humidity in the environment. The symptoms are termed as shedding of flowers. This is due to adverse environmental factors.

# 8

# Symptoms caused by Physiological Disorders

The physiological changes in plant occur due to deficiency or excess of essential or non-essential elements. Infertile soil, poor light, excess of temperature, excess of water or sacristy of water induces physiological disorder in plants. The physiological disorders in plants are expressed in the form of various types of symptoms. Certain types of symptoms caused by physiological disorder in plants are discussed below.

Symptoms caused by physiological disorders in plants are as follows:

1. Tip burn
2. Albino
3. Chlorosis
4. Marginal flavescence
5. Watery fruit
6. Black heart
7. Whip tail
8. Cresting
9. Pinking
10. Bitterness
11. Frost
12. Legginess
13. Silvering
14. Blossom end rot
15. Puffiness
16. Sterility
17. Spongy tissue
18. Black tip

## Tip Burn

The leaves of affected plant start drying from tip region. The drying extends downward along the margin resulting in the drying of complete leaf. In severe cases entire plant becomes leafless because of defoliation of affected leaves. Exm: Tip burn of paddy. The causal agent is not properly understood, (Dastur, 1937). Tip burn of mango (physiological disorder). The tip burn extends gradually causing drying and death of leaf. Defoliation affects the yield of plant. Tip burn initially affects the photosynthetic area of leaf (Bhat, 2013).

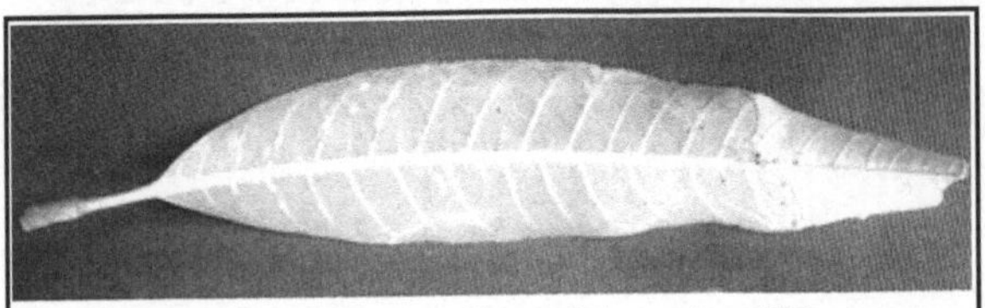

**Tip Burn of Mango: Causal Agent not Known**

## Albino

The leaves are green in colour due to presence of chlorophyll. The chlorophyll contain chlorophyll-a, chlorophyll-b, xanthophylls, and carotene. Lacks of any one of pigment out of these four produce white coloured leaves. The albino symptoms of leaf adversely affect the process of photosynthesis. Development of albino symptoms of leaves is the physiological disorder of plant.

**Albino Symptoms in Plants**

## Chlorosis

The reduced functioning of chlorophyll results into a various kinds of chlorosis. The chlorosis may be due to mineral deficiency, viral disease, wilt, or any other agencies. Chlorosis may takes place in the form of patches or streaks or entire leaf or whole plant sometimes shows chlorosis.

### Marginal Flavescence

It is very common types of symptom occur in certain vegetables and herbaceous plants. The infected plant possesses leaves with chlorotic margins. The infected plant remains short, stunted, it appears like a bush. Such a bushy stunted plant produces very less flowers. The symptoms affect the photosynthetic area of the leaf. Such types of symptoms are termed as marginal flavescence which is caused due to infection of phytoplasma or mineral deficiency, (Bhat, 2013).

### Watery Fruit

Water quantity in the fruit is increased due to an excessive root pressure in the affected plant. This is a physiological disorder, which increase the volume of cells and sometimes damage them, hence the pulp of fruit turn watery. The symptoms are termed as watery fruit. Shelf life of such fruits is very much short and such fruits are highly susceptible for secondary infections of specific bacterial and fungal pathogens.

### Black Heart

It is a symptom with highly specific characteristics. In case of black heart of potato, the tuber develops and its normal size but internally it is black when cut open, into two, pieces. The blacking started from the centre and gradually forwarded towards the outward region. The blackening of internal tissue may be uniform or appear star shaped. The affect tissue may be soft or slightly leathery. A fully affected tuber gets rotted and shrinked off. The shrinkage of potato sometimes creates central hallow, which is surrounded by black tissue. Hence the disease symptoms termed black heart,( Bhat, 2013). A black spot may develop on affected potato which later turns to black wound, through which secondary infection takes place. Black heart of tubers caused due to insufficient oxygen. So it is a physiological disorder of potato tubers.

### Whip Tail

A variety of courses responsible for whip tail symptoms of cauliflower. It is a physiological disorder. Warning *et.al.*, (1949) reported the cause of whip tail is molybdenum. The characteristics features of whip tail are extension and growth of leaf lamina to tail like structure which is long, flexible like a whip, growing point do not produce normal head (cauliflower) it is highly deformed. At the base of plant these sprouts are farmed. Such type of symptoms termed as whip tail.

### Cresting

The cresting is the symptoms which represents the fusion of stem and buds in the form of flattened masses. The cause of such type of symptoms in the affected plant may be living or non-living entity.

### Pinking

Due to exposure of growing heads of cauliflower synthesis of anthocyanin; such types of symptoms are rarely developed.

### Bitterness

The characteristic features of symptoms are the affected carrot becomes bitter in taste. This is caused due to production of ethylene which increases total phenol content of carrots, the bitterness of carrot reduces quality and such carrots are unfit for consumption.

### Frost

Blackish patches are developed on the bracts around the floral axis which later wilt. Such symptoms are termed as artichoke frost. Such types of symptoms are observed in Artichoke vegetable this is a physiological disorder.

### Legginess

The affected tuber produces a very long and thin sprouts; this is due to physiological disorder caused due to excess heating of tubers. Such type of symptoms termed as legginess.

### Silvering

When the leaf epidermis of infected plant turn to grayish silver coloured which is somewhat shining in appearance. The region is light reflective. These types of symptoms are caused due to biochemical abnormality in plants or insect activity. Such types of symptoms are termed as silvering.

### Blossom End Rot

Blossom end rot symptoms are commonly observed in most of the fruits and vegetable crops. It is caused due to physiological disorder like unfavourable humidity, root health and pH of soil. The sign of infection initiates at the blossom eng region of affected fruit. The affected fruits remain small and solid. At the blossom end region a proteinaceous growth is seen at the initial stage and gradually disorganisation of tissue results into a tough necrosis. The affected region get shrinked and dry up. A depressed area becomes clearly distinct. During full maturity of such rot disease. Winsor and Adams (1987) reported correlation of blossom end rot diseases with calcium concentration of fruits.

### Puffiness

The fruits of tomato possess hollow space inside. The hollow space or cavity formation takes place between the outer wall and the locular contents. The affected fruit appear angular in shape. The hollow space is developed due to restricted or slow growth of internal tissue of tomato. Whereas the outer wall develop normally. Because of hollow cavity formation inside the fruit, the fruit becomes light in weight. The affected fruits are not firm and that are partially filled. The affected fruits are very soft, angular and flat. According to Grierson and Kader (1986) the cause of puffiness in tomato fruits is due to genetical disorder. Yarnell, *et.al.*, (1937) reported the reason of puffiness in tomato is due to disturbances in normal metabolism.

### Sterility

The infected plant does not produce fruits and seeds due to interaction of pathogen with host or any physiological or biochemical or genetically disorder. Such type of abnormality in plants is termed as sterility and the plant is termed as sterile. The symptom is also termed as abortion.

### Spongy Tissue

The symptoms mostly occur on fruits. The affected fruits show spongy development in the flesh. The fruits emit bad odour and which becomes unfit for consumption. Spongy tissue symptoms of mango in caused due to physiological disorder.

### Black Tip

Due to physiological disorder the tip of fruits like mango turn dark black in colour. Initially a small, etiolated area develops at the distal end of the fruit which spreads and covers the whole tip. The tip becomes flattened and the skin turns hard and sunken. The black tip symptoms on mango fruit occur due to physiological disorder. Black tip is common in those fruits which are about to the maturity.

### Symptomatology of Mineral Deficiency (Essential and Non-essential Elements in Plants)

The minerals which are essential for the growth and development of plants are Boron Calcium, Iron, Magnesium, Manganese, Nitrogen, Phosphorous, Potassium etc. The nutrients are non- infectious. The important minerals which are essential for growth of plants and the diseases caused by deficiency or excess of a particular element are discussed below.

Plants contain about 40 different elements. Some of them are necessary for normal growth and development of plant and called as essential elements. Rest of the elements are called as non-essential elements.

Essential elements are as follows: Carbon (C), Hydrogen (H), Oxygen (O), Nitrogen (N), Phosphorus (P), Potassium (K), Calcium (Ca), Sulphur (S), Magnesium (Mg), Iron (Fe), Manganese (Mn), Zinc (Zn), Boron (Br), Copper (Cu), & Mo (Molybdenum). Besides this Aluminium (Al), Silicon (Si), Chlorine (Cl), Sodium (Na), Cobalt (Co), Gallium (Ga) are essential elements.

Essential elements may be classified into two groups. i.e. Major elements (Macro-nutrients) and Minor elements (Micro-nutrients or trace elements). The essential elements which are required by the plants in comparatively large amount are called as major elements or macronutrient. They are C, H, O, N, P, K, Ca, S, Mg, and Fe. The essential elements which are required are very small amount or traces by the plants are called as minor elements or (micronutrients). Trace elements are usually radioactive or heavy isotopes which are used to trace out some metabolic pathway such as $C^{14}$, $N^{15}$, $O^{18}$, $P^{32}$, $S^{35}$, and K42 & $Ca^{45}$.

## Importance of Macro Elements

1. **Nitrogen** is important constituent of protein, amino acids, nucleic acid prophyrin, alkaloids, some vitamins, co-enzymes etc. Prophyrin are important part of chlorophylls and cytochromes. Nitrogen plays very important role in metabolism growth, reproduction heredity, photosynthesis and respiration.
2. **Phosphorous:** It is important constituents of nucleic acids phospholipids, co-enzymes, NAD, NADP & ATP etc. Phospholipids along with proteins may be important constituents of cell membranes. Through nucleic acid and ATP it plays important role in protein synthesis. Through co-enzymes NAD, NADP, ATP it plays an important role in oxidation reduction and energy transfer reaction of cell metabolism e.g. photosynthesis, respiration and fat metabolism act.
3. **Sulphur:** It is important constituent of some amino acids. Disulphide linkages help to stabilize the protein structure. It is also constituent of vitamins, biotin, thiamine and co-enzymes A. Sulphur is constituent of ferrodoxin and of some lipids found in chloroplast.
4. **Calcium:** It is important constituent of the middle lamella in cell wall. It is essential in the formation of cell membranes. It helps to stabilize the structure of the chromosomes. It may be an activator for many enzymes. Calcium has many roles in the structure & metabolism

of plants. Calcium helps in the translocation of carbohydrates & amino acids and encourages root development.

5. **Magnesium:** It is very important constituent of chlorophylls. It acts as activator for many enzymes in phosphate transfer reaction particularly in carbohydrates metabolism and nucleic acids synthesis. It plays important role in binding ribosome particles during protein synthesis. It plays an important role in synthesis of ATP from ADP & inorganic phosphate.
6. **Potassium:** It is essential for the process of respiration and photosynthesis.

   It acts as activator of many enzymes involved in carbohydrate metabolism and protein synthesis. It is essential in maintaining the cellular organization, Permeability osmotic potential of plant cells and turgor.
7. **Iron:** It is important constituent of iron Prophyrin etc proteins like cytochromes peroxidases, catalases etc. It is essential for the synthesis of chlorophyll. It is very important constituent of ferrodoxin which plays important role in biological nitrogen fixation and primary photochemical reaction in photosynthesis. It play important role in respiratory mechanism. Iron is a component of several electron carriers.

**Importance of Micronutrients (minor or trace elements)**

1. **Manganese:** It is activator of many respiratory enzymes. It is also an activator of the enzymes nitrite reductase and hydroxylamine reductase. It is necessary for the evolution of oxygen during photosynthesis. It also plays some role in the synthesis of chlorophyll.
2. **Copper:** It is constituent of several oxidizing enzymes acts as a catalyst. Their higher concentrations are toxic to plants. The elements are required in very small quantity. It is part of plastocyanin and helps in electron transport chain of photosynthesis.
3. **Zinc:** It is involved in the biosynthesis of the growth hormone Auxin, Indole, 3 acetic acid (IAA). It acts as

activator of many enzymes like carbonic anhydrase alcohol-dehydrogenase, hexose kinase. It is concerned with protein metabolism and chlorophyll synthesis.

4. **Boron:** It facilitates the translocation of sugars in plants. It promotes synthesis of nucleic acid and elongation of the cell. It also plays an important role in the function of membranes.
5. **Molybdenum:** It is associated with the prosthetic group of the enzyme nitrate reductase nitrogenase and thus plays important role in nitrogen metabolism. Its ions are activators of several enzymes. It is required in very little quantity in the plants.

### Symptoms Caused by Nutrient Deficiency in Plants

The stunting growth, burning of leaves, yellowing and defoliation or discoloration of affected plant parts is commonly seen in the plants due to shortage or excess of the necessary nutrients. Such diseases of plants occur when the soil is less fertile or lost fertility. To make soil healthy for the growth of plants adds plenty of well-rotted organic matter to the soil by this method, the diseases of plants caused by nutrient deficiency can be controlled.

**Green banding:** In certain vegetable crops, the vein banding occurs when there is a bond of dark green tissue along the larger veins of the leaf. Such type of changes in leaf is termed as green banding. The green banding in vegetable crop is caused by mineral deficiency.

### Symptoms Caused by Nitrogen Deficiency

Nitrogen (N) is a very important constituent of protein, amino acids, enzymes hormone, chlorophyll and vitamins. The nitrogen deficiency in plants show stunted growth, woody stems, yellowing or browning of leaves. Such plants show sugar accumulation in the tissue; flowering and fruiting may be delayed. All vegetables apart from nitrogen fixing legumes are susceptible to this disorder.

The control of nitrogen deficiency can be achieved by using grass mowing as mulch or foliar feeding with manure or by using nitrogen rich fertilizers such as urea, ammonium nitrate or humus.

Nitrogen deficiency causes, yellowing i.e. chlorosis of leaves, older leavers are affected first.

In many plants e.g. Tomato the stem, Petiole and the leaf veins become coloured due to anthocyanin pigments. Plant growth is stunted because protein content cell division and cell enlargement are decreased. Early defoliation of plant suppressed shoot growth. The flowering is delayed.

(a) **Pithiness:** The petioles of affected leafy vegetable made up of this walled parenchyma cells. Pithiness is the breakdown of leaf petiole. This is caused due to excess dose of nitrogen fertilizer. Exm: Celery Petioles.

(b) **Splitting:** The symptoms splitting are characterized by cracking of affected fruits or carrots. Splitting symptoms are commonly observed in carrot. (Wallace, et.al, 1942). It is caused to nitrogen deficiency. The split on pen or cracked carrots get infected by a variety of other organisms. Due to secondary infection, the affected carrots become unfit for consumption.

**Symptoms Caused by Phosphorus Deficiency in Plants**

Phosphorous (P) deficiencies in plant occur commonly in areas of high rainfall, especially on acid, clay or poor chalk soil. This is an uncommon disorder. The susceptible crops are carrot, lettuce, spinach, apple, currents and amla. Symptoms include poor growth; leaves turn blue or green but not yellow. Oldest leaves found more susceptible. Fruits become small and acid testing. Phosphorus is a constituent of phospholipids nucleic acids and many proteins. It is essential in carbohydrate transformation and respiration. Phosphorous is involved in high energy bonding.

The deficient cotton plants are dwarfed and their foliage turn dark green. The highly susceptible plants are pitches fruits and flex. It can be controlled by applying organic sources of phosphorous such as rock phosphate. The application of phosphate fertilizers controls the disease.

Phosphorus deficiency may cause premature leaf fall dead necrotic areas may be developed on leaves or fruits. Leaves made turn dark to blue green in colour. The growth of root and shoot is extremely restricted. Flowering is delayed. Branching is sparse.

(a) **Pencil Stripe:** The infected plant shows narrow brown lines on surface of leaf petioles. Such symptoms termed as pencil stripe. Exm: Celery petioles. This is caused due to high soil phosphorus content.

**Symptoms caused by Sulfur Deficiency (S) in Plants**

Leaves show uniform yellowing no spots develop on it.Sulphur deficiency cause yellowing (i.e. chlorosis) of the leaves tips and margin of the leaf, roll in ward, stem become hard due to the development of sclerenchyma. Sulphur deficiency results in shortage of protein causing stunted growth.

**Symptoms caused by Potassium Deficiency (K) in Plants**

The plants require potassium ions ($K^+$) for protein synthesis and for the opening and closing of stomata. Plants need potassium in large amount. It is also essential for photosynthesis and cambial activity. The susceptible crops are potatoes, tobacco, cotton forage, legumes, and other crop plants which require large quantity of potassium.

The potassium deficient plant of shows mild chlorosis, browning of tips of leaves, yellowing of interveinal tissues, browning of laminar tissue and necrotic spots are seen in alfalfa and clover.

The potassium deficiency diseases can be controlled by using potassium rich fertilizers or by adding plenty of well-rotted compost or manure to the soil. Wood ash has high potassium content, which can be used.

Mottled chlorosis of leaves occurs necrotic areas develop at the tip and margins of the leaf which curve downward. Plant growth remains stunted with marked shortening of internodes. Scorching of older leaves is important symptoms on fruit trees. The stem become thin, weak and leaves exhibit curling.

**Symptoms caused by Boron Deficiency (B)**

Boron deficiency is a rare disorder affecting plants growing above granite bedrock, which is low in boron. Boron may be present but locked up in soils with a high pH. The deficiency may be worse in wet season. The symptoms include drying of growing tips, and bushy stunted growth.

Boron deficiency causes death of the shoot tip flower formation is suppressed. The root tip die, root growth is stunted leave become coppery in texture. Necrosis of the apices, fruits fleshy roots, tuber, young leaves. It inhibits cell division and nitrogenase.

### *Diseases of Boron Deficiency*

Diseases of boron deficiency are as follows:

(a) **Beetroot:** Rough cankered patches on roots, internal brown rot of beetroot.

(b) **Cabbage:** Distorted leaves, hollow areas in stems.

(c) **Cauliflower:** Poor development of plant and brown patches on leaf. The stems, leafstalk, and midrib roughened.

(d) **Strawberries:** Stunted growth, foliage small yellow and puckered at tips, fruits are small and pale.

(e) **Palm tree:** Brown spots on fronds and lower productivity.

Boron deficiency can be avoided by improving the moisture retaining capacity of light soils and ensuring pH is kept below 7. Boron can be ranked into the soil at $35 g/m^2$.

(f) **Brown Heart:** The characteristics features of brown heart symptoms are, the young unfolding leaves fails to develop normally and gradually the entire plant turn rough and brown. Plant appears unhealthy. The roots turn grey.Such symptoms termed as brown heart. It is caused due to boron deficiency in soil.

(g) **Hollow Stem**: Hollow stem symptoms are developed in most of the economically important plants due to boron deficiency, in cole vegetable. The characteristics features of hollow stem symptoms are rolling and curling of leaves, browning of flowers and hollow stem centers.

**(h) Sickle leaf**

The infected leaf possesses interveinal chlorosis, it appears in patches and in severe cases of disease development the green portion is found around the sides of the veins giving vein banding appearance. Later on the leaves show mottling and crinkling with wavy margin. The younger leaves reduce to a greater extent and appear sickle shaped. The yield is greatly reduced. Such type of symptoms can be observed in cocoa due to deficiency of boron.

### Symptoms caused by Calcium Deficiency in Plants

Calcium (Ca) deficiency is a plant disorder that can be caused by insufficient calcium in the growing medium but it is more frequently a product of a compromised nutrient mobility system in the plant. This may be due to water shortage, which slow the transpiration of calcium to the plant or can be caused by excessive usage of potassium or nitrogen fertilizers.

Calcium deficiency symptoms appear initially as stunted plant growth, necrotic leaf margins on young leaves or curling of the leaves and eventual death of terminal buds and root tips. Generally the new growth of the plant is affected first. The mature leaves may be affected if the problem persists.

Exm: Apple shows bitter pit, fruit skin develops pits, brown patches appear in flesh and taste becomes bitter. It can occur during storage. Cabbage shows cavity spot which are oval. Tomato shows sunken dry decaying areas at the blossom end of the fruit, sometimes blossom end rot occurs. Calcium deficiency can be recorrected by adding agricultural lime to acid soils.

Calcium deficiency causes disintegration of growing meristematic regions of the root, stem and leaves. Chlorosis occurs along the margins of the younger leaves. Malformation of younger leaves also takes places. Calcium deficiency results in necrosis of young leaves. The plants may be stunted.

(a) **Golden specks:** According to Den Outer and Van Veenendaal (1988) a very small granular particle of calcium oxide crystals' which are golden yellow in colour which occur close to the blossom end region of tomato. This affects the price of fruits. Such types of symptoms are termed as golden specks.

(b) **Hypocotyls necrosis:** The affected seedling possesses necrotic spots on hypocotyls region. The necrotic spot contain dead tissue. Such types of symptom develop due to deficiency of calcium in soil.

(c) **Black heart:** Initially due to deficiency of calcium the deeply seated tissue of celery stem turn dark black in colour which gradually spread deeply through the stem. The young leaves show tip burn symptoms. Plant dries up. In severe cases of disease development the killing of entire plant is common.

### Symptoms caused by Iron Deficiency in Plants

Iron (Fe) deficiency is a plant disorder also known as lime induced chlorosis. A deficiency in the soil is rare. Iron can be unavailable if pH is too high or if the soil is water logged. Any plant may be affected but raspberries and pears are particularly susceptible as well as most acid loving plants. Deficient plant show yellowing of leaves or browning of leaves in margins between the veins which may remains green, while young leaves may appear to be bleached. The fruits show poor quality.

Iron deficiency can be recovered by choosing appropriate soil for the growing conditions. Iron deficiency can be caused by acidic conditions.

Iron deficiency causes rapid chlorosis of the leaves which is usually interveinal. The symptoms appear first in the younger leaves.

### Symptoms caused by Magnesium deficiency in plants

Magnesium (Mg) deficiency is a plant disorder with two main causes. Magnesium can be easily washed out from light soils in wet seasons or excessive potassium fertilizer usage can cause Mg to become unavailable to the growing plant. The disorder particularly affects potatoes, tomatoes, apples, currants, gooseberries and chrysanthemums.

Symptoms include yellowing between leaves. The veins remain green, giving a marveled appearance. This begins with older leaves and spreads to younger growth. Fruits remain small and woody.

Magnesium deficiency causes interveinal chlorosis of the leaves, the order leaves are affected first dead necrotic patches and anthocyanin pigment appear on the leaves. The leaves show premature leaf abscission.

### Symptoms caused by Manganese Deficiency

Manganese (Mn) deficiency is a plant disorder that is often confused with and occurs with iron deficiency. Most common in poorly drained soils, also where organic matter levels are high. Manganese may be unavailable to plants where pH is higher.

Tip Burn of Mango

Affected plants include onion, apple, pea, French beans, cherry and raspberry and symptoms include yellowing of leaves with smallest leaf veins remaining green to produce a check board effect. Brown spots may appear on leaf surfaces and severely affected leaves turn brown and wither. Manganese deficiency causes chlorotic and necrotic spots in the interveinal areas of the leaf. The leaf takes mottled appearance. Grey spots appear on the leaves and in the grains of oat.

### Symptoms caused by Copper Deficiency

Copper deficiency causes necrosis of the tip of the young leaves. It also causes die-back of citrus and other trees and reclamation disease of cereals and leguminous plants.

### Symptoms caused by Zinc Deficiency

Zinc deficiency causes chlorosis of the older leaves which starts from tips and the margins it causes mottle leaves disease in apple, citrus, walnut and other fruit trees. Leaves show white necrotic spots. It suppresses seed formation and causes malformation in fruiting trees.

### Symptoms caused by Molybdenum deficiency

It causes chlorotic interveinal mottling of older leaves flower formation is inhibited. It causes whip tail disease in cauliflower plants. The leaves become twisted and ultimately die.

(a) **Albinism:** Albinism is a type of symptoms of physiological disorder. In this observed in strawberry fruits at maturity due to mineral deficiency. The affected fruit have poor flavor. Fruits do not ripe uniformly, and show wary appearance. Such fruit are highly susceptible for secondary infection of storage fungi.

**(b) Whip tail:** Whip tail symptoms develop in turnip due to deficiency of Molybdenum. An acidic soil favors the disease. In this case, infected plant possesses narrow leaves, cupped down, showing deep chlorotic patches, mottling around the margins. The roots stop the growth. such type of adverse effect in plants is termed as whip tail.

### Symptoms caused by Adverse Effect of Ethylene

Especially in the post-harvest fruits & vegetables ethylene increases the rate of respiration, alters the activity of enzymes and permeability of cell wall of perishable increases. Ethylene stress causes cellular changes. Loss of quality such as change in colour, flavor and texture takes place.In healthy green colour of vegetables ethylene has been shown to increase degradation of chlorophyll and yellowing of vegetable (Poenicke, *et.al.*, 1977). Exposure of carrots to ethylene increased phenolics (Sarkar &Phan, 1979). Ethylene also causes change in the texture of commodity. Ethylene is used for ripening of fruits in the markets of India. Hatton (1982) reported that there is marked increase in toughness of commodity due to exposure to ethylene.

# References


Agrios, George (2005). *Plant Pathology.* Academic Press. ISBN 978-0-12-044565-3.

Alexopoulos, C.J. and Mims, C.W., (1979). *Introductory Mycology.* 3rd Edn. New Delhi, India.

Ali, S.M. & Dennis, J., (1992). Host Range and Physiological Specialization of Macrophomina Phaseolina Isolated from Fields Pea in South Australia. *Australian Journal of Experimental Agriculture* 32, 1121-1125.

Arias, R.S., Ray, J.D., Mengistu, A. & Scheffler, B.E., (2011). Discriminating Microsatellites from Macrophomina Phaseolina and Their Potential Association to Biological Functions. *Plant Pathology* 60, 709-718.

Arnold, D.L., Pitman, A., and Jackson, R.W. (2003). Pathogenicity and Other Genomic Islands in Plant Pathogenic Bacteria. *Mol. Plant Pathol.* 4: 407-420.

Arneson, P.A., (2001). "Plant Disease Epidemiology: Temporal Aspects". *Plant Health Instructor* (American Phytopathological Society). doi: 10.1094/PHI-A-2001-0524-01.

Arthur, J.C. (1885). Proof that the Disease of Trees Known as Pear Blight is Directly due to Bacteria. N.Y. *Agric. Exp. St. Bull.* 2 n.s: 1-4.

Babu, C., (2010). Pre-breeding in Sugarcane (*Saccharum* sp. Hybrids) for Red Rot Resistance and Economic Traits. *Electronic Journal of Plant Breeding*, 1(4): 1024-1034.

Bellaloui, N., Mengistu, A. & Paris, R.L., (2008). Soybean Seed Composition in Cultivars Differing in Resistance to Charcoal Rot (*Macrophomina phaseolina*). *Journal of Agricultural Science*, Cambridge 146, 667-675.

Bengtsson M., Hockenhull, J. & de Neergaard, E. (2006). Histopathological Study of the Effect of Post Leaf Fall Application of Urea on Saprotrophic Development of the Cherry Leaf Spot Pathogen, *Blumeriella jaapii.* Journal of *Plant Diseases and Protection*, 113 (5): 214-218.

Bertamini, M; Grando, M. S. and Nedunchezhian, N. (2004). "Effects of Phytoplasma Infection on Pigments, Chlorophyll-Protein Complex and Photosynthetic Activities in Field Grown Apple Leaves". *Biologia Plantarum* (Springer Netherlands) 47 (2): 237-242.

Bhat, K.L., ( 2013). *Physiological Disorders of Vegetable Crops.* Daya Publishing House, Astral International Pvt.Ltd. Delhi, pp. 12-140.

Burrill, Thomas Jonathan. (1878). *Pear Blight.* Trans III. State Hort. Soc. 114-116.

Cao, H., Baldini, R.L. and Rahme, L.G. (2001). Common Mechanisms for Pathogens of Plants and Animals. *Annu. Rev. Phytopathol.* 39: 259-284.

Chen, X.M., (2005). Epidemiology and Control of Stripe Rust [*Puccinia striiformis* f. sp. *tritici*] on Wheat. *Canadian Journal of Plant Pathology* 27, 314-337.

Cooke, B.M., D.G. Jones and B. Kaye, (ed.) *The Epidemiology of Plant Diseases,* New York: Springer, 2006.

de Vallavieille-Pope C, Ali S, Leconte M, Enjalbert J, Delos M, Rouzet J. (2012). Virulence Dynamics and Regional Structuring of *Puccinia striiformis* f. sp *tritici* in France Between 1984 and 2009. *Plant Disease* 96: 131-140.

de Armas R, Santiago R, Legaz ME, Vicente C. (2007) Levels of Phenolic Compounds and Enzyme Activity can be

Used to Screen for Resistance of Sugarcane to Smut (*Ustilago scitaminea*). *Australasian Plant Pathology*, 2007; 36: 32-38.

Dhingra, O.D. & Sinclair, J. B. (1978). Biology and Pathology of Macrophomina Phaseolina. Viçosa, Brazil: Imprensa Universitária, Universidade Federal de Viçosa.

Drenth, A., (2004). "Fungal Epidemics – does Spatial Structure Matter?". *New Phytologist* (Blackwells) 163 (1): 4-7.

Farr, D.F. & A.Y. Rossman, (2012). Fungal Databases, Systematic Mycology and Microbiology Laboratory, ARS, USDA.

Fatima, Sumia, Avinash Ade and Zafar Javeed, (2006). *Post Harvest Rots of Fruits*, Discovery Publishing House Pvt. Ltd., New Delhi.

Glawe, D.A., (2008). The Powdery Mildews: A Review of the World's most Familiar (Yet Poorly known) Plant Pathogens. *Annual Review of Phytopathology* 46: 27-51.

Grabowski, M. (June 1, 2012). *Cold Wet Soils Help Root Rotting Fungi*. University of Minnesota Extension. Retrieved June 3, 2012.

Hodson, *et.al.*, "Tracking the Wheat Rust Pathogens". (2012). Borlaug Global Rust Initiative Technical Workshop Proceedings. Borlaug Global Rust Initiative. Retrieved 28 November 2012.

Holb, I. (2009): Some Biological Features of Cherry Leaf Spot (*Blumeriella jaapii*) with Special Reference to cultisvar Susceptibility *International Journal of Horticultural Science*, 15 (1-2): 91-94.

Jin, Y., Szabo, L. J., and M. Carson. (2010). Century-old Mystery of *Puccinia striiformis* Life History Solved with Identification of *Berberis* as an Alternate Host. *Phytopathology*. 100: 432-435.

Khurana, S.M.P. and Singh (1973). *Hort. Abstr.* 43: 9.

Keitt, G.W., Blodgett, E.C., Wilson, E.E. & Magie, R.O. (1937): The Epidemiology and Control of Cherry Leaf Spot. Univ. *Wisc. Agric. Exp. Stn. Res. Bull.*, 132.

Khan, S.N. (2007). *Macrophomina phaseolina* as Causal Agent for Charcoal Rot of Sunflower. Mycopathology 5, 111-118.

Krishna, A. and R.A. Singh, 1983. Longevity of Teliospores of *Neovossia indica* Causing Karnal Bunt of Wheat. *Indian J. Mycol. Pl. Pathol.*,13: 97-8.

Kumar Bijender and Rashmi Yadav, (2012). Influence of Nitrogen Fertilizer Dose on Blast Disease of Finger Millet Caused by *Pyricularia grisea. Indian Phytopath.* 1: 52-55.

Lee, IM; Davis RE and Gundersen-Rindal DE (2000). "Phytoplasma: Phytopathogenic Mollicutes". *Annual Review of Microbiology* (Annual Reviews) 54: 221-255.

Mansoor, S., Briddon, R.W. Zafar, Y., Stanley, J., (March 2003). "Geminivirus Disease Complexes: An Emerging Threat". *Trends Plant Sci.*

Mansoor, S., I. Amin, S. Iram, M. Hussain, Y. Zafar, K.A. Malik, and R.W. Briddon. (2003a). The Breakdown of Resistance in Cotton to Cotton Leaf Curl Disease in Pakistan. *Plant Pathol.* 52: 784.

Marsalis, M. & Goldberg, N., (2006). *Leaf, Stem, and Stripe Rust Diseases of Wheat.* [Fact sheet]. New Mexico State University.

Marwat, Sarfaraz Khan, Mir Ajab Khan, Muhammad Aslam Khan, Mushtaq Ahmad, Muhammad Zafar, Fazal-ur-Rehman and Shazia Sultana (2009). "Vegetables Mentioned in the Holy Qura'n and Ahadith and Their Ethnomedicinal Studies in Dera Ismail Khan, N.W.F.P., Pakistan". *Pakistan Journal of Nutrition* 8 (5): 530-538.

McManus, P., Sundin, G., Proffer, T., Berardi, R., Ma, Z. & Ehret, G. (2005): Integration of Copper, Strobilurin, and Sterol Demethylation Inhibitor Fungicides for Control of Cherry Leaf Spot. (Abstr.) *Phytopathology*, 95: S68.

Mishra, B. & Sinha, S.K. (1982). Studies on Wilt of Linseed Caused by Rhizoctonia Bataticola. *Indian Phytopathology*, 35, 555-557.

Mohanan,C., (2010). *Rust Fungi of Kerala.* India, Kerala Forest Research Institute. p. 148. ISBN 81-85041-72-5.

Munjal, R.L., V.V Chenulu, and I.S. Hora, (1963). Assessment of Losses due to Powdery Muldew *Erysiphe polygoni* on Pea. *Indian Phytopath.*, 16: 260-267.

Mundkur, B.B., 1940. A Second Contribution Towards a Knowledge of Indian Ustilaginales. *Trans. British Mycol.* Soc., 24: 312-36.

Narasimha, S. Rao, K. Ravindra Kumar & M. Anandaraaj, (2012). Management of Leaf Spot of Turmeric (*Curcuma longa* L.) Incited by *Colletotrichum capsici* Through Fungicides, *Journal of Spices and Aromatic Crops*, Vol. 21 (2): 151-154.

Papademetriou Manis K. (Ed.) (2008). Workshop to Commemorate the International Year of the Potato - 2008. FAO-RAP, Bangkok Thailand 6 May 2008.

Pataky, J.K., and K.M. Snetselaar. (2006). Common Smut of Corn. The Plant Health Instructor.

Patel, M.H., M.J. Thirumalachar, M.V. Desai, and M.K. Patel. (1959). An Improved Method of Testing the Longevity of Spores of *Tolyposporium penicillariae* Bref. in Soil. *Current Science* 28: 28-29.

Phadtare, G.G., and K.P. Sharma. (1971). Additional Hosts of *Synchytriurn endobioticurn. Indian Phytopathology* 24: 38 9-3 92.

Pegg, G.F. and Brady, B.L. (2002). *Verticillium Wilts*, CABI Publishing, New York, NY.

Pockman, W.T.; J.S. Sperry and J.W. O'Leary (December 1995). "Sustained and Significant Negative Water Pressure in Xylem". *Nature* 378 (6558): 715-6.

Que, Y.X.; Lin, J.W., Zhang, J.S., Ruan, M.H., Xu, L.P., Zhang, M.Q. (2008). Molecular Cloning and Characterization of a Non-TIR-NBS-LRR Type Disease Resistance Gene Analogue from Sugarcane. *Sugar Tech*, Vol. 10, pp. 71-73.

Ramezani, M., Shier, W.*T., Abbas, H.K., Tono*s, J.L., Baids, R.E. & Sciumbato, G.L. (2007). Soybean Charcoal Rot Disease Fungus *Macrophomina phaseolina* in Mississippi

Produces the Phytotoxin (–)-botryodiplodin but no Detectable Phaseolinone. *Journal of Natural Products* 70, 128-129.

Ramakrishnan, T.S. (1942). A Leaf Spot Disease of *Zingiber officinale* Caused by *Phyllosticta zingiber. Proc. Indian Acad. Sci.* 15: 167-171.

Rathore, B.S. (2006). Management of Diseases of Green Gram with Fungicides. *Indian Journal of Mycology and Plant Pathology* 36: 138-141.

Rawat, B.S. and A.K. Saxena, ( 1990). A Note on the Natural Population Levels of Short-nosed Cattle Louse *Linognathus vituli* (Linne). *Rivista di Parassitologia*, Vol. VII (LI), NW, AGOSTO, 183-188.

Reed, C.; S. Doyungan; B. Ioerger; A. Gretchell (2007). "Response of Storage Molds to Different Initial Moisture Contents of Maize(corn) Stored at 25 C, and Effect on Respiration Rate and Nutrient Composition". *Journal of Stored Products Research* 43: 443-458.

Rekha Kumari, K.S., Shekhawat Renu Gupta and M.K. Khokhar, (2012). Integrated Management Against Root-rot of Mungbean [*Vigna radiate* (L.) Wilczek] Incited by Macrophomina Phaseolina, J. Plant Pathol. Microb., 3: 5.

Rimmer, S.R. and van der Berg, C.G.J. (2007). Black Leg (Phoma Stem Canker). pp. 19-22 in *Compendium of Brassica Diseases.* S.R. Rimmer, V.I. Shattuck, and L. Buchwaldt (eds.). St. Paul, MN: APS Press.

Ryder, M.H. and Jones, D.A. (1991). *Biological Control of Crown Gall Using Santiago.*

R., de Armas, R., Legaz, M.-E. & Vicente, C. (2008). Separation from *Ustilago Scitaminea* of Different Elicitors which Modify the Pattern of Phenolic Accumulation in Sugarcane Leaves. *Journal of Plant Pathology*, Vol. 90, No. 1, pp. 87-96.

San-Blas G; Calderone RA (editors). (2008). *Pathogenic Fungi.* Caister Academic Press. ISBN 978-1-904455-32-5.

Schmidt, H. & Gruppe, W. (1988): Breeding Dwarfing Rootstocks for Sweet Cherries. *Hort Science*, 23: 112-114.

Scarito, G., Salamone, A., Zizzo, G.V., Agnello, S. ( 2007). Use of Natural Products for the Control of Powdery Mildew of Rose Plants. *Acta Horticulturae* 751: 251-257.

Schumann, G. & D'Arcy, C. (2010). *Essential Plant Pathology.* APS Press.

Singh, R.S., (1998). *Plant Disease.* 7th ed. Oxford and IBH Publishing Co., New Delhi.

Singh,K., (1998), "Grossy Shoot Disease of Sugarcane-II: Hot Air Therapy" *Curr. Sci.* 37: 592-594.

Singh, R. P., D.P. Hodson, J. Huerta-Espino, *et.al.*, (2008). Will Stem Rust Destroy the World's Wheat Crop? *Adv. Agronomy* 98: 271-309.

Srivastava, H.P., (1985). Some Leaf Spot Fungi. Proc. *Natl. Acad. Sci.*, 34B:188.

"Stone, (2010) - Box Office Mojo". *Box Office Mojo.* Retrieved October 17, 2010.

Sutton, B.C.; Waller, J.M. (1988). Taxonomy of *Ophiocladium hordei,* Causing Leaf Lesions on Triticale and Other Gramineae. *Trans. Brit. Mycol. Soc.* 90 (1): 55-61.

Shirshikar, S.P., (2008). Integrated Management of Sunflower Necrosis Disease. *HELIA*, 31, Nr. 49, pp. 27-34.

Takimoto, S., (1920). [On the bacterial leaf-spot of *Antirrhinum majus* L.] *Botanical Magazine Tokyo* 34, 253-257.

Thakur, R.P., Shetty, H.S. and Khairwal, I.S., (2006). Pearl Millet Downy Mildew Research in India: Progress and Perspectives. *International Sorghum and Millets Newsletter* 47: 125-130.

Thakur, P.D., Anil Kumar, Sharma, Usha and Handa, Anil, ( 2006). Serological Detection of Apple Chlorotic Leaf Spot Virus in Different Parts of an Apple Tree. *Plant Disease Research*, 21(1): 19-21.

Townshend, J.L. and T.R. Davidson. (1960). Some Weed Hosts of *Pratylenchus penetrans* in Premier Strawberry Plantations. *Canadian Journal of Botany* 38: 267-273.

Tredway Lane, P., et.al, (2011). "Damping Off ( *Pythium & Rhizoctonia spp.*". North Carolina State University; Turf Files Environmental Research and Education (center).

Warham, E.J., 1984. A Comparison of Inoculation Methods for Karnal Bunt *Neovossia Indica. Phytopathology,* 74: 856-7.

Watt, B.A.,( 2010). Black Spot of Rose. University of Maine, *Pest Management Fact Sheet* #5907.

Webster, J. and R.W.S. Weber. (2007). *Introduction to Fungi.* Cambridge University Press, New York.

White, M.M., T.Y. James, K. O'Donnell, M.J. Cafaro, Y. Tanabe, and J. Sugiyama. ( 2006). Phylogeny of the Zygomycota Based on Nuclear Ribosomal Sequence data. *Mycologia* 98: 872-884.

William Surman, (19 August 2010). "Major New Disease Threat to Potatoes". Farmers Guardian/UBM *Information Ltd. Retrieved* 26 July 2011.

Willits, D.A. and J.E. Sherwood. (1999). Polymerase Chain Reaction Detection of *Ustilago hordei* in Leaves of Susceptible and Resistant Barley Varieties. Phytopathology 89: 212-217.

*www.nzffa.org.nz/farm.../the.../resinosis-on-agathis-australis-kauri/*

www.hawaiiplantdisease.net/glossary/ Hydrosis_(water_soakin). htm.

Zieslin, N and A.H. Halevy (28 APR 2006). *Flower Bud Atrophy in Baccara Roses.* Volume 37, Issue 4, pages 331–335, August 1976.

Zhang, P., McIntosh, R., Hoxha, S., Bansal, U., (2012). The Relationship of Lr13 and Hybrid Necrosis Gene Ne2m. *Borlaug Global Rust Initiative 2012 Technical Workshop,* Beijing: Borlaug Global Rust Initiative.

# Index

T



V



W



X



Z



◆ ◆ ◆ ◆ ◆ ◆